C-3525 CAREER EXAMINATION SERIES

This is your
PASSBOOK for...

Car Appearance Supervisor

Test Preparation Study Guide
Questions & Answers

COPYRIGHT NOTICE

This book is SOLELY intended for, is sold ONLY to, and its use is RESTRICTED to individual, bona fide applicants or candidates who qualify by virtue of having seriously filed applications for appropriate license, certificate, professional and/or promotional advancement, higher school matriculation, scholarship, or other legitimate requirements of education and/or governmental authorities.

This book is NOT intended for use, class instruction, tutoring, training, duplication, copying, reprinting, excerption, or adaptation, etc., by:

1) Other publishers
2) Proprietors and/or Instructors of "Coaching" and/or Preparatory Courses
3) Personnel and/or Training Divisions of commercial, industrial, and governmental organizations
4) Schools, colleges, or universities and/or their departments and staffs, including teachers and other personnel
5) Testing Agencies or Bureaus
6) Study groups which seek by the purchase of a single volume to copy and/or duplicate and/or adapt this material for use by the group as a whole without having purchased individual volumes for each of the members of the group
7) Et al.

Such persons would be in violation of appropriate Federal and State statutes.

PROVISION OF LICENSING AGREEMENTS – Recognized educational, commercial, industrial, and governmental institutions and organizations, and others legitimately engaged in educational pursuits, including training, testing, and measurement activities, may address request for a licensing agreement to the copyright owners, who will determine whether, and under what conditions, including fees and charges, the materials in this book may be used them. In other words, a licensing facility exists for the legitimate use of the material in this book on other than an individual basis. However, it is asseverated and affirmed here that the material in this book CANNOT be used without the receipt of the express permission of such a licensing agreement from the Publishers. Inquiries re licensing should be addressed to the company, attention rights and permissions department.

All rights reserved, including the right of reproduction in whole or in part, in any form or by any means, electronic or mechanical, including photocopying, recording, or by any information storage and retrieval system, without permission in writing from the Publisher.

Copyright © 2024 by
National Learning Corporation

212 Michael Drive, Syosset, NY 11791
(516) 921-8888 • www.passbooks.com
E-mail: info@passbooks.com

PUBLISHED IN THE UNITED STATES OF AMERICA

PASSBOOK® SERIES

THE *PASSBOOK® SERIES* has been created to prepare applicants and candidates for the ultimate academic battlefield – the examination room.

At some time in our lives, each and every one of us may be required to take an examination – for validation, matriculation, admission, qualification, registration, certification, or licensure.

Based on the assumption that every applicant or candidate has met the basic formal educational standards, has taken the required number of courses, and read the necessary texts, the *PASSBOOK® SERIES* furnishes the one special preparation which may assure passing with confidence, instead of failing with insecurity. Examination questions – together with answers – are furnished as the basic vehicle for study so that the mysteries of the examination and its compounding difficulties may be eliminated or diminished by a sure method.

This book is meant to help you pass your examination provided that you qualify and are serious in your objective.

The entire field is reviewed through the huge store of content information which is succinctly presented through a provocative and challenging approach – the question-and-answer method.

A climate of success is established by furnishing the correct answers at the end of each test.

You soon learn to recognize types of questions, forms of questions, and patterns of questioning. You may even begin to anticipate expected outcomes.

You perceive that many questions are repeated or adapted so that you can gain acute insights, which may enable you to score many sure points.

You learn how to confront new questions, or types of questions, and to attack them confidently and work out the correct answers.

You note objectives and emphases, and recognize pitfalls and dangers, so that you may make positive educational adjustments.

Moreover, you are kept fully informed in relation to new concepts, methods, practices, and directions in the field.

You discover that you are actually taking the examination all the time: you are preparing for the examination by "taking" an examination, not by reading extraneous and/or supererogatory textbooks.

In short, this PASSBOOK®, used directedly, should be an important factor in helping you to pass your test.

CAR APPEARANCE SUPERVISOR

JOB DESCRIPTION
Performs supervisory work related to the enhancement of the appearance of subway cars and associated facilities. May supervise personnel engaged in the repair of subway cars and associated equipment. Performs such related work and duties as the transit authority is authorized by law to prescribe in its regulation.

SCOPE OF THE EXAMINATION
The written test will be of the multiple-choice type and may include questions on: car cleaning and enhancement procedures; specialized machinery, tools and equipment; safe work practices and basic first aid procedures; job-related computations; supervisory methods and techniques in accordance with the rules and regulations of the transit authority; and other related matters.

HOW TO TAKE A TEST

I. YOU MUST PASS AN EXAMINATION

A. *WHAT EVERY CANDIDATE SHOULD KNOW*

Examination applicants often ask us for help in preparing for the written test. What can I study in advance? What kinds of questions will be asked? How will the test be given? How will the papers be graded?

As an applicant for a civil service examination, you may be wondering about some of these things. Our purpose here is to suggest effective methods of advance study and to describe civil service examinations.

Your chances for success on this examination can be increased if you know how to prepare. Those "pre-examination jitters" can be reduced if you know what to expect. You can even experience an adventure in good citizenship if you know why civil service exams are given.

B. *WHY ARE CIVIL SERVICE EXAMINATIONS GIVEN?*

Civil service examinations are important to you in two ways. As a citizen, you want public jobs filled by employees who know how to do their work. As a job seeker, you want a fair chance to compete for that job on an equal footing with other candidates. The best-known means of accomplishing this two-fold goal is the competitive examination.

Exams are widely publicized throughout the nation. They may be administered for jobs in federal, state, city, municipal, town or village governments or agencies.

Any citizen may apply, with some limitations, such as the age or residence of applicants. Your experience and education may be reviewed to see whether you meet the requirements for the particular examination. When these requirements exist, they are reasonable and applied consistently to all applicants. Thus, a competitive examination may cause you some uneasiness now, but it is your privilege and safeguard.

C. *HOW ARE CIVIL SERVICE EXAMS DEVELOPED?*

Examinations are carefully written by trained technicians who are specialists in the field known as "psychological measurement," in consultation with recognized authorities in the field of work that the test will cover. These experts recommend the subject matter areas or skills to be tested; only those knowledges or skills important to your success on the job are included. The most reliable books and source materials available are used as references. Together, the experts and technicians judge the difficulty level of the questions.

Test technicians know how to phrase questions so that the problem is clearly stated. Their ethics do not permit "trick" or "catch" questions. Questions may have been tried out on sample groups, or subjected to statistical analysis, to determine their usefulness.

Written tests are often used in combination with performance tests, ratings of training and experience, and oral interviews. All of these measures combine to form the best-known means of finding the right person for the right job.

II. HOW TO PASS THE WRITTEN TEST

A. NATURE OF THE EXAMINATION

To prepare intelligently for civil service examinations, you should know how they differ from school examinations you have taken. In school you were assigned certain definite pages to read or subjects to cover. The examination questions were quite detailed and usually emphasized memory. Civil service exams, on the other hand, try to discover your present ability to perform the duties of a position, plus your potentiality to learn these duties. In other words, a civil service exam attempts to predict how successful you will be. Questions cover such a broad area that they cannot be as minute and detailed as school exam questions.

In the public service similar kinds of work, or positions, are grouped together in one "class." This process is known as *position-classification*. All the positions in a class are paid according to the salary range for that class. One class title covers all of these positions, and they are all tested by the same examination.

B. FOUR BASIC STEPS

1) Study the announcement

How, then, can you know what subjects to study? Our best answer is: "Learn as much as possible about the class of positions for which you've applied." The exam will test the knowledge, skills and abilities needed to do the work.

Your most valuable source of information about the position you want is the official exam announcement. This announcement lists the training and experience qualifications. Check these standards and apply only if you come reasonably close to meeting them.

The brief description of the position in the examination announcement offers some clues to the subjects which will be tested. Think about the job itself. Review the duties in your mind. Can you perform them, or are there some in which you are rusty? Fill in the blank spots in your preparation.

Many jurisdictions preview the written test in the exam announcement by including a section called "Knowledge and Abilities Required," "Scope of the Examination," or some similar heading. Here you will find out specifically what fields will be tested.

2) Review your own background

Once you learn in general what the position is all about, and what you need to know to do the work, ask yourself which subjects you already know fairly well and which need improvement. You may wonder whether to concentrate on improving your strong areas or on building some background in your fields of weakness. When the announcement has specified "some knowledge" or "considerable knowledge," or has used adjectives like "beginning principles of..." or "advanced ... methods," you can get a clue as to the number and difficulty of questions to be asked in any given field. More questions, and hence broader coverage, would be included for those subjects which are more important in the work. Now weigh your strengths and weaknesses against the job requirements and prepare accordingly.

3) Determine the level of the position

Another way to tell how intensively you should prepare is to understand the level of the job for which you are applying. Is it the entering level? In other words, is this the position in which beginners in a field of work are hired? Or is it an intermediate or advanced level? Sometimes this is indicated by such words as "Junior" or "Senior" in the class title. Other jurisdictions use Roman numerals to designate the level – Clerk I, Clerk II, for example. The word "Supervisor" sometimes appears in the title. If the level is not indicated by the title, check the description of duties. Will you be working under very close supervision, or will you have responsibility for independent decisions in this work?

4) Choose appropriate study materials

Now that you know the subjects to be examined and the relative amount of each subject to be covered, you can choose suitable study materials. For beginning level jobs, or even advanced ones, if you have a pronounced weakness in some aspect of your training, read a modern, standard textbook in that field. Be sure it is up to date and has general coverage. Such books are normally available at your library, and the librarian will be glad to help you locate one. For entry-level positions, questions of appropriate difficulty are chosen – neither highly advanced questions, nor those too simple. Such questions require careful thought but not advanced training.

If the position for which you are applying is technical or advanced, you will read more advanced, specialized material. If you are already familiar with the basic principles of your field, elementary textbooks would waste your time. Concentrate on advanced textbooks and technical periodicals. Think through the concepts and review difficult problems in your field.

These are all general sources. You can get more ideas on your own initiative, following these leads. For example, training manuals and publications of the government agency which employs workers in your field can be useful, particularly for technical and professional positions. A letter or visit to the government department involved may result in more specific study suggestions, and certainly will provide you with a more definite idea of the exact nature of the position you are seeking.

III. KINDS OF TESTS

Tests are used for purposes other than measuring knowledge and ability to perform specified duties. For some positions, it is equally important to test ability to make adjustments to new situations or to profit from training. In others, basic mental abilities not dependent on information are essential. Questions which test these things may not appear as pertinent to the duties of the position as those which test for knowledge and information. Yet they are often highly important parts of a fair examination. For very general questions, it is almost impossible to help you direct your study efforts. What we can do is to point out some of the more common of these general abilities needed in public service positions and describe some typical questions.

1) General information

Broad, general information has been found useful for predicting job success in some kinds of work. This is tested in a variety of ways, from vocabulary lists to questions about current events. Basic background in some field of work, such as sociology or economics, may be sampled in a group of questions. Often these are principles which have become familiar to most persons through exposure rather than through formal training. It is difficult to advise you how to study for these questions; being alert to the world around you is our best suggestion.

2) Verbal ability

An example of an ability needed in many positions is verbal or language ability. Verbal ability is, in brief, the ability to use and understand words. Vocabulary and grammar tests are typical measures of this ability. Reading comprehension or paragraph interpretation questions are common in many kinds of civil service tests. You are given a paragraph of written material and asked to find its central meaning.

3) Numerical ability

Number skills can be tested by the familiar arithmetic problem, by checking paired lists of numbers to see which are alike and which are different, or by interpreting charts and graphs. In the latter test, a graph may be printed in the test booklet which you are asked to use as the basis for answering questions.

4) Observation

A popular test for law-enforcement positions is the observation test. A picture is shown to you for several minutes, then taken away. Questions about the picture test your ability to observe both details and larger elements.

5) Following directions

In many positions in the public service, the employee must be able to carry out written instructions dependably and accurately. You may be given a chart with several columns, each column listing a variety of information. The questions require you to carry out directions involving the information given in the chart.

6) Skills and aptitudes

Performance tests effectively measure some manual skills and aptitudes. When the skill is one in which you are trained, such as typing or shorthand, you can practice. These tests are often very much like those given in business school or high school courses. For many of the other skills and aptitudes, however, no short-time preparation can be made. Skills and abilities natural to you or that you have developed throughout your lifetime are being tested.

Many of the general questions just described provide all the data needed to answer the questions and ask you to use your reasoning ability to find the answers. Your best preparation for these tests, as well as for tests of facts and ideas, is to be at your physical and mental best. You, no doubt, have your own methods of getting into an exam-taking mood and keeping "in shape." The next section lists some ideas on this subject.

IV. KINDS OF QUESTIONS

Only rarely is the "essay" question, which you answer in narrative form, used in civil service tests. Civil service tests are usually of the short-answer type. Full instructions for answering these questions will be given to you at the examination. But in case this is your first experience with short-answer questions and separate answer sheets, here is what you need to know:

1) Multiple-choice Questions

Most popular of the short-answer questions is the "multiple choice" or "best answer" question. It can be used, for example, to test for factual knowledge, ability to solve problems or judgment in meeting situations found at work.

A multiple-choice question is normally one of three types—
- It can begin with an incomplete statement followed by several possible endings. You are to find the one ending which *best* completes the statement, although some of the others may not be entirely wrong.
- It can also be a complete statement in the form of a question which is answered by choosing one of the statements listed.

- It can be in the form of a problem – again you select the best answer.

Here is an example of a multiple-choice question with a discussion which should give you some clues as to the method for choosing the right answer:

When an employee has a complaint about his assignment, the action which will *best* help him overcome his difficulty is to
- A. discuss his difficulty with his coworkers
- B. take the problem to the head of the organization
- C. take the problem to the person who gave him the assignment
- D. say nothing to anyone about his complaint

In answering this question, you should study each of the choices to find which is best. Consider choice "A" – Certainly an employee may discuss his complaint with fellow employees, but no change or improvement can result, and the complaint remains unresolved. Choice "B" is a poor choice since the head of the organization probably does not know what assignment you have been given, and taking your problem to him is known as "going over the head" of the supervisor. The supervisor, or person who made the assignment, is the person who can clarify it or correct any injustice. Choice "C" is, therefore, correct. To say nothing, as in choice "D," is unwise. Supervisors have and interest in knowing the problems employees are facing, and the employee is seeking a solution to his problem.

2) True/False Questions

The "true/false" or "right/wrong" form of question is sometimes used. Here a complete statement is given. Your job is to decide whether the statement is right or wrong.

SAMPLE: A roaming cell-phone call to a nearby city costs less than a non-roaming call to a distant city.

This statement is wrong, or false, since roaming calls are more expensive.

This is not a complete list of all possible question forms, although most of the others are variations of these common types. You will always get complete directions for answering questions. Be sure you understand *how* to mark your answers – ask questions until you do.

V. RECORDING YOUR ANSWERS

Computer terminals are used more and more today for many different kinds of exams.

For an examination with very few applicants, you may be told to record your answers in the test booklet itself. Separate answer sheets are much more common. If this separate answer sheet is to be scored by machine – and this is often the case – it is highly important that you mark your answers correctly in order to get credit.

An electronic scoring machine is often used in civil service offices because of the speed with which papers can be scored. Machine-scored answer sheets must be marked with a pencil, which will be given to you. This pencil has a high graphite content which responds to the electronic scoring machine. As a matter of fact, stray dots may register as answers, so do not let your pencil rest on the answer sheet while you are pondering the correct answer. Also, if your pencil lead breaks or is otherwise defective, ask for another.

Since the answer sheet will be dropped in a slot in the scoring machine, be careful not to bend the corners or get the paper crumpled.

The answer sheet normally has five vertical columns of numbers, with 30 numbers to a column. These numbers correspond to the question numbers in your test booklet. After each number, going across the page are four or five pairs of dotted lines. These short dotted lines have small letters or numbers above them. The first two pairs may also have a "T" or "F" above the letters. This indicates that the first two pairs only are to be used if the questions are of the true-false type. If the questions are multiple choice, disregard the "T" and "F" and pay attention only to the small letters or numbers.

Answer your questions in the manner of the sample that follows:

32. The largest city in the United States is
    A. Washington, D.C.
    B. New York City
    C. Chicago
    D. Detroit
    E. San Francisco

1) Choose the answer you think is best. (New York City is the largest, so "B" is correct.)
2) Find the row of dotted lines numbered the same as the question you are answering. (Find row number 32)
3) Find the pair of dotted lines corresponding to the answer. (Find the pair of lines under the mark "B.")
4) Make a solid black mark between the dotted lines.

VI. BEFORE THE TEST

Common sense will help you find procedures to follow to get ready for an examination. Too many of us, however, overlook these sensible measures. Indeed, nervousness and fatigue have been found to be the most serious reasons why applicants fail to do their best on civil service tests. Here is a list of reminders:

- Begin your preparation early – Don't wait until the last minute to go scurrying around for books and materials or to find out what the position is all about.
- Prepare continuously – An hour a night for a week is better than an all-night cram session. This has been definitely established. What is more, a night a week for a month will return better dividends than crowding your study into a shorter period of time.
- Locate the place of the exam – You have been sent a notice telling you when and where to report for the examination. If the location is in a different town or otherwise unfamiliar to you, it would be well to inquire the best route and learn something about the building.
- Relax the night before the test – Allow your mind to rest. Do not study at all that night. Plan some mild recreation or diversion; then go to bed early and get a good night's sleep.
- Get up early enough to make a leisurely trip to the place for the test – This way unforeseen events, traffic snarls, unfamiliar buildings, etc. will not upset you.
- Dress comfortably – A written test is not a fashion show. You will be known by number and not by name, so wear something comfortable.

- Leave excess paraphernalia at home – Shopping bags and odd bundles will get in your way. You need bring only the items mentioned in the official notice you received; usually everything you need is provided. Do not bring reference books to the exam. They will only confuse those last minutes and be taken away from you when in the test room.
- Arrive somewhat ahead of time – If because of transportation schedules you must get there very early, bring a newspaper or magazine to take your mind off yourself while waiting.
- Locate the examination room – When you have found the proper room, you will be directed to the seat or part of the room where you will sit. Sometimes you are given a sheet of instructions to read while you are waiting. Do not fill out any forms until you are told to do so; just read them and be prepared.
- Relax and prepare to listen to the instructions
- If you have any physical problem that may keep you from doing your best, be sure to tell the test administrator. If you are sick or in poor health, you really cannot do your best on the exam. You can come back and take the test some other time.

VII. AT THE TEST

The day of the test is here and you have the test booklet in your hand. The temptation to get going is very strong. Caution! There is more to success than knowing the right answers. You must know how to identify your papers and understand variations in the type of short-answer question used in this particular examination. Follow these suggestions for maximum results from your efforts:

1) Cooperate with the monitor

The test administrator has a duty to create a situation in which you can be as much at ease as possible. He will give instructions, tell you when to begin, check to see that you are marking your answer sheet correctly, and so on. He is not there to guard you, although he will see that your competitors do not take unfair advantage. He wants to help you do your best.

2) Listen to all instructions

Don't jump the gun! Wait until you understand all directions. In most civil service tests you get more time than you need to answer the questions. So don't be in a hurry. Read each word of instructions until you clearly understand the meaning. Study the examples, listen to all announcements and follow directions. Ask questions if you do not understand what to do.

3) Identify your papers

Civil service exams are usually identified by number only. You will be assigned a number; you must not put your name on your test papers. Be sure to copy your number correctly. Since more than one exam may be given, copy your exact examination title.

4) Plan your time

Unless you are told that a test is a "speed" or "rate of work" test, speed itself is usually not important. Time enough to answer all the questions will be provided, but this does not mean that you have all day. An overall time limit has been set. Divide the total time (in minutes) by the number of questions to determine the approximate time you have for each question.

5) Do not linger over difficult questions

If you come across a difficult question, mark it with a paper clip (useful to have along) and come back to it when you have been through the booklet. One caution if you do this – be sure to skip a number on your answer sheet as well. Check often to be sure that you have not lost your place and that you are marking in the row numbered the same as the question you are answering.

6) Read the questions

Be sure you know what the question asks! Many capable people are unsuccessful because they failed to *read* the questions correctly.

7) Answer all questions

Unless you have been instructed that a penalty will be deducted for incorrect answers, it is better to guess than to omit a question.

8) Speed tests

It is often better NOT to guess on speed tests. It has been found that on timed tests people are tempted to spend the last few seconds before time is called in marking answers at random – without even reading them – in the hope of picking up a few extra points. To discourage this practice, the instructions may warn you that your score will be "corrected" for guessing. That is, a penalty will be applied. The incorrect answers will be deducted from the correct ones, or some other penalty formula will be used.

9) Review your answers

If you finish before time is called, go back to the questions you guessed or omitted to give them further thought. Review other answers if you have time.

10) Return your test materials

If you are ready to leave before others have finished or time is called, take ALL your materials to the monitor and leave quietly. Never take any test material with you. The monitor can discover whose papers are not complete, and taking a test booklet may be grounds for disqualification.

VIII. EXAMINATION TECHNIQUES

1) Read the general instructions carefully. These are usually printed on the first page of the exam booklet. As a rule, these instructions refer to the timing of the examination; the fact that you should not start work until the signal and must stop work at a signal, etc. If there are any *special* instructions, such as a choice of questions to be answered, make sure that you note this instruction carefully.

2) When you are ready to start work on the examination, that is as soon as the signal has been given, read the instructions to each question booklet, underline any key words or phrases, such as *least, best, outline, describe* and the like. In this way you will tend to answer as requested rather than discover on reviewing your paper that you *listed without describing*, that you selected the *worst* choice rather than the *best* choice, etc.

3) If the examination is of the objective or multiple-choice type – that is, each question will also give a series of possible answers: A, B, C or D, and you are called upon to select the best answer and write the letter next to that answer on your answer paper – it is advisable to start answering each question in turn. There may be anywhere from 50 to 100 such questions in the three or four hours allotted and you can see how much time would be taken if you read through all the questions before beginning to answer any. Furthermore, if you come across a question or group of questions which you know would be difficult to answer, it would undoubtedly affect your handling of all the other questions.

4) If the examination is of the essay type and contains but a few questions, it is a moot point as to whether you should read all the questions before starting to answer any one. Of course, if you are given a choice – say five out of seven and the like – then it is essential to read all the questions so you can eliminate the two that are most difficult. If, however, you are asked to answer all the questions, there may be danger in trying to answer the easiest one first because you may find that you will spend too much time on it. The best technique is to answer the first question, then proceed to the second, etc.

5) Time your answers. Before the exam begins, write down the time it started, then add the time allowed for the examination and write down the time it must be completed, then divide the time available somewhat as follows:
    - If 3-1/2 hours are allowed, that would be 210 minutes. If you have 80 objective-type questions, that would be an average of 2-1/2 minutes per question. Allow yourself no more than 2 minutes per question, or a total of 160 minutes, which will permit about 50 minutes to review.
    - If for the time allotment of 210 minutes there are 7 essay questions to answer, that would average about 30 minutes a question. Give yourself only 25 minutes per question so that you have about 35 minutes to review.

6) The most important instruction is to *read each question* and make sure you know what is wanted. The second most important instruction is to *time yourself properly* so that you answer every question. The third most important instruction is to *answer every question*. Guess if you have to but include something for each question. Remember that you will receive no credit for a blank and will probably receive some credit if you write something in answer to an essay question. If you guess a letter – say "B" for a multiple-choice question – you may have guessed right. If you leave a blank as an answer to a multiple-choice question, the examiners may respect your feelings but it will not add a point to your score. Some exams may penalize you for wrong answers, so in such cases *only*, you may not want to guess unless you have some basis for your answer.

7) Suggestions
   a. Objective-type questions
      1. Examine the question booklet for proper sequence of pages and questions
      2. Read all instructions carefully
      3. Skip any question which seems too difficult; return to it after all other questions have been answered
      4. Apportion your time properly; do not spend too much time on any single question or group of questions

5. Note and underline key words – *all, most, fewest, least, best, worst, same, opposite*, etc.
6. Pay particular attention to negatives
7. Note unusual option, e.g., unduly long, short, complex, different or similar in content to the body of the question
8. Observe the use of "hedging" words – *probably, may, most likely*, etc.
9. Make sure that your answer is put next to the same number as the question
10. Do not second-guess unless you have good reason to believe the second answer is definitely more correct
11. Cross out original answer if you decide another answer is more accurate; do not erase until you are ready to hand your paper in
12. Answer all questions; guess unless instructed otherwise
13. Leave time for review

   b. Essay questions
     1. Read each question carefully
     2. Determine exactly what is wanted. Underline key words or phrases.
     3. Decide on outline or paragraph answer
     4. Include many different points and elements unless asked to develop any one or two points or elements
     5. Show impartiality by giving pros and cons unless directed to select one side only
     6. Make and write down any assumptions you find necessary to answer the questions
     7. Watch your English, grammar, punctuation and choice of words
     8. Time your answers; don't crowd material

8) Answering the essay question

Most essay questions can be answered by framing the specific response around several key words or ideas. Here are a few such key words or ideas:

M's: manpower, materials, methods, money, management
P's: purpose, program, policy, plan, procedure, practice, problems, pitfalls, personnel, public relations

   a. Six basic steps in handling problems:
     1. Preliminary plan and background development
     2. Collect information, data and facts
     3. Analyze and interpret information, data and facts
     4. Analyze and develop solutions as well as make recommendations
     5. Prepare report and sell recommendations
     6. Install recommendations and follow up effectiveness

   b. Pitfalls to avoid
     1. *Taking things for granted* – A statement of the situation does not necessarily imply that each of the elements is necessarily true; for example, a complaint may be invalid and biased so that all that can be taken for granted is that a complaint has been registered

2. *Considering only one side of a situation* – Wherever possible, indicate several alternatives and then point out the reasons you selected the best one
3. *Failing to indicate follow up* – Whenever your answer indicates action on your part, make certain that you will take proper follow-up action to see how successful your recommendations, procedures or actions turn out to be
4. *Taking too long in answering any single question* – Remember to time your answers properly

IX. AFTER THE TEST

Scoring procedures differ in detail among civil service jurisdictions although the general principles are the same. Whether the papers are hand-scored or graded by machine we have described, they are nearly always graded by number. That is, the person who marks the paper knows only the number – never the name – of the applicant. Not until all the papers have been graded will they be matched with names. If other tests, such as training and experience or oral interview ratings have been given, scores will be combined. Different parts of the examination usually have different weights. For example, the written test might count 60 percent of the final grade, and a rating of training and experience 40 percent. In many jurisdictions, veterans will have a certain number of points added to their grades.

After the final grade has been determined, the names are placed in grade order and an eligible list is established. There are various methods for resolving ties between those who get the same final grade – probably the most common is to place first the name of the person whose application was received first. Job offers are made from the eligible list in the order the names appear on it. You will be notified of your grade and your rank as soon as all these computations have been made. This will be done as rapidly as possible.

People who are found to meet the requirements in the announcement are called "eligibles." Their names are put on a list of eligible candidates. An eligible's chances of getting a job depend on how high he stands on this list and how fast agencies are filling jobs from the list.

When a job is to be filled from a list of eligibles, the agency asks for the names of people on the list of eligibles for that job. When the civil service commission receives this request, it sends to the agency the names of the three people highest on this list. Or, if the job to be filled has specialized requirements, the office sends the agency the names of the top three persons who meet these requirements from the general list.

The appointing officer makes a choice from among the three people whose names were sent to him. If the selected person accepts the appointment, the names of the others are put back on the list to be considered for future openings.

That is the rule in hiring from all kinds of eligible lists, whether they are for typist, carpenter, chemist, or something else. For every vacancy, the appointing officer has his choice of any one of the top three eligibles on the list. This explains why the person whose name is on top of the list sometimes does not get an appointment when some of the persons lower on the list do. If the appointing officer chooses the second or third eligible, the No. 1 eligible does not get a job at once, but stays on the list until he is appointed or the list is terminated.

X. HOW TO PASS THE INTERVIEW TEST

The examination for which you applied requires an oral interview test. You have already taken the written test and you are now being called for the interview test – the final part of the formal examination.

You may think that it is not possible to prepare for an interview test and that there are no procedures to follow during an interview. Our purpose is to point out some things you can do in advance that will help you and some good rules to follow and pitfalls to avoid while you are being interviewed.

What is an interview supposed to test?

The written examination is designed to test the technical knowledge and competence of the candidate; the oral is designed to evaluate intangible qualities, not readily measured otherwise, and to establish a list showing the relative fitness of each candidate – as measured against his competitors – for the position sought. Scoring is not on the basis of "right" and "wrong," but on a sliding scale of values ranging from "not passable" to "outstanding." As a matter of fact, it is possible to achieve a relatively low score without a single "incorrect" answer because of evident weakness in the qualities being measured.

Occasionally, an examination may consist entirely of an oral test – either an individual or a group oral. In such cases, information is sought concerning the technical knowledges and abilities of the candidate, since there has been no written examination for this purpose. More commonly, however, an oral test is used to supplement a written examination.

Who conducts interviews?

The composition of oral boards varies among different jurisdictions. In nearly all, a representative of the personnel department serves as chairman. One of the members of the board may be a representative of the department in which the candidate would work. In some cases, "outside experts" are used, and, frequently, a businessman or some other representative of the general public is asked to serve. Labor and management or other special groups may be represented. The aim is to secure the services of experts in the appropriate field.

However the board is composed, it is a good idea (and not at all improper or unethical) to ascertain in advance of the interview who the members are and what groups they represent. When you are introduced to them, you will have some idea of their backgrounds and interests, and at least you will not stutter and stammer over their names.

What should be done before the interview?

While knowledge about the board members is useful and takes some of the surprise element out of the interview, there is other preparation which is more substantive. It *is* possible to prepare for an oral interview – in several ways:

1) Keep a copy of your application and review it carefully before the interview

This may be the only document before the oral board, and the starting point of the interview. Know what education and experience you have listed there, and the sequence and dates of all of it. Sometimes the board will ask you to review the highlights of your experience for them; you should not have to hem and haw doing it.

2) Study the class specification and the examination announcement

Usually, the oral board has one or both of these to guide them. The qualities, characteristics or knowledges required by the position sought are stated in these documents. They offer valuable clues as to the nature of the oral interview. For example, if the job involves supervisory responsibilities, the announcement will usually indicate that knowledge of modern supervisory methods and the qualifications of the candidate as a supervisor will be tested. If so, you can expect such questions, frequently in the form of a hypothetical situation which you are expected to solve. NEVER go into an oral without knowledge of the duties and responsibilities of the job you seek.

3) Think through each qualification required

Try to visualize the kind of questions you would ask if you were a board member. How well could you answer them? Try especially to appraise your own knowledge and background in each area, *measured against the job sought*, and identify any areas in which you are weak. Be critical and realistic – do not flatter yourself.

4) Do some general reading in areas in which you feel you may be weak

For example, if the job involves supervision and your past experience has NOT, some general reading in supervisory methods and practices, particularly in the field of human relations, might be useful. Do NOT study agency procedures or detailed manuals. The oral board will be testing your understanding and capacity, not your memory.

5) Get a good night's sleep and watch your general health and mental attitude

You will want a clear head at the interview. Take care of a cold or any other minor ailment, and of course, no hangovers.

What should be done on the day of the interview?

Now comes the day of the interview itself. Give yourself plenty of time to get there. Plan to arrive somewhat ahead of the scheduled time, particularly if your appointment is in the fore part of the day. If a previous candidate fails to appear, the board might be ready for you a bit early. By early afternoon an oral board is almost invariably behind schedule if there are many candidates, and you may have to wait. Take along a book or magazine to read, or your application to review, but leave any extraneous material in the waiting room when you go in for your interview. In any event, relax and compose yourself.

The matter of dress is important. The board is forming impressions about you – from your experience, your manners, your attitude, and your appearance. Give your personal appearance careful attention. Dress your best, but not your flashiest. Choose conservative, appropriate clothing, and be sure it is immaculate. This is a business interview, and your appearance should indicate that you regard it as such. Besides, being well groomed and properly dressed will help boost your confidence.

Sooner or later, someone will call your name and escort you into the interview room. *This is it.* From here on you are on your own. It is too late for any more preparation. But remember, you asked for this opportunity to prove your fitness, and you are here because your request was granted.

What happens when you go in?

The usual sequence of events will be as follows: The clerk (who is often the board stenographer) will introduce you to the chairman of the oral board, who will introduce you to the other members of the board. Acknowledge the introductions before you sit down. Do not be surprised if you find a microphone facing you or a stenotypist sitting by. Oral interviews are usually recorded in the event of an appeal or other review.

Usually the chairman of the board will open the interview by reviewing the highlights of your education and work experience from your application – primarily for the benefit of the other members of the board, as well as to get the material into the record. Do not interrupt or comment unless there is an error or significant misinterpretation; if that is the case, do not hesitate. But do not quibble about insignificant matters. Also, he will usually ask you some question about your education, experience or your present job – partly to get you to start talking and to establish the interviewing "rapport." He may start the actual questioning, or turn it over to one of the other members. Frequently, each member undertakes the questioning on a particular area, one in which he is perhaps most competent, so you can expect each member to participate in the examination. Because time is limited, you may also expect some rather abrupt switches in the direction the questioning takes, so do not be upset by it. Normally, a board member will not pursue a single line of questioning unless he discovers a particular strength or weakness.

After each member has participated, the chairman will usually ask whether any member has any further questions, then will ask you if you have anything you wish to add. Unless you are expecting this question, it may floor you. Worse, it may start you off on an extended, extemporaneous speech. The board is not usually seeking more information. The question is principally to offer you a last opportunity to present further qualifications or to indicate that you have nothing to add. So, if you feel that a significant qualification or characteristic has been overlooked, it is proper to point it out in a sentence or so. Do not compliment the board on the thoroughness of their examination – they have been sketchy, and you know it. If you wish, merely say, "No thank you, I have nothing further to add." This is a point where you can "talk yourself out" of a good impression or fail to present an important bit of information. Remember, *you close the interview yourself.*

The chairman will then say, "That is all, Mr. _____, thank you." Do not be startled; the interview is over, and quicker than you think. Thank him, gather your belongings and take your leave. Save your sigh of relief for the other side of the door.

How to put your best foot forward

Throughout this entire process, you may feel that the board individually and collectively is trying to pierce your defenses, seek out your hidden weaknesses and embarrass and confuse you. Actually, this is not true. They are obliged to make an appraisal of your qualifications for the job you are seeking, and they want to see you in your best light. Remember, they must interview all candidates and a non-cooperative candidate may become a failure in spite of their best efforts to bring out his qualifications. Here are 15 suggestions that will help you:

1) Be natural – Keep your attitude confident, not cocky

If you are not confident that you can do the job, do not expect the board to be. Do not apologize for your weaknesses, try to bring out your strong points. The board is interested in a positive, not negative, presentation. Cockiness will antagonize any board member and make him wonder if you are covering up a weakness by a false show of strength.

2) Get comfortable, but don't lounge or sprawl

Sit erectly but not stiffly. A careless posture may lead the board to conclude that you are careless in other things, or at least that you are not impressed by the importance of the occasion. Either conclusion is natural, even if incorrect. Do not fuss with your clothing, a pencil or an ashtray. Your hands may occasionally be useful to emphasize a point; do not let them become a point of distraction.

3) Do not wisecrack or make small talk

This is a serious situation, and your attitude should show that you consider it as such. Further, the time of the board is limited – they do not want to waste it, and neither should you.

4) Do not exaggerate your experience or abilities

In the first place, from information in the application or other interviews and sources, the board may know more about you than you think. Secondly, you probably will not get away with it. An experienced board is rather adept at spotting such a situation, so do not take the chance.

5) If you know a board member, do not make a point of it, yet do not hide it

Certainly you are not fooling him, and probably not the other members of the board. Do not try to take advantage of your acquaintanceship – it will probably do you little good.

6) Do not dominate the interview

Let the board do that. They will give you the clues – do not assume that you have to do all the talking. Realize that the board has a number of questions to ask you, and do not try to take up all the interview time by showing off your extensive knowledge of the answer to the first one.

7) Be attentive

You only have 20 minutes or so, and you should keep your attention at its sharpest throughout. When a member is addressing a problem or question to you, give him your undivided attention. Address your reply principally to him, but do not exclude the other board members.

8) Do not interrupt

A board member may be stating a problem for you to analyze. He will ask you a question when the time comes. Let him state the problem, and wait for the question.

9) Make sure you understand the question

Do not try to answer until you are sure what the question is. If it is not clear, restate it in your own words or ask the board member to clarify it for you. However, do not haggle about minor elements.

10) Reply promptly but not hastily

A common entry on oral board rating sheets is "candidate responded readily," or "candidate hesitated in replies." Respond as promptly and quickly as you can, but do not jump to a hasty, ill-considered answer.

11) Do not be peremptory in your answers

A brief answer is proper – but do not fire your answer back. That is a losing game from your point of view. The board member can probably ask questions much faster than you can answer them.

12) Do not try to create the answer you think the board member wants

He is interested in what kind of mind you have and how it works – not in playing games. Furthermore, he can usually spot this practice and will actually grade you down on it.

13) Do not switch sides in your reply merely to agree with a board member

Frequently, a member will take a contrary position merely to draw you out and to see if you are willing and able to defend your point of view. Do not start a debate, yet do not surrender a good position. If a position is worth taking, it is worth defending.

14) Do not be afraid to admit an error in judgment if you are shown to be wrong

The board knows that you are forced to reply without any opportunity for careful consideration. Your answer may be demonstrably wrong. If so, admit it and get on with the interview.

15) Do not dwell at length on your present job

The opening question may relate to your present assignment. Answer the question but do not go into an extended discussion. You are being examined for a *new* job, not your present one. As a matter of fact, try to phrase ALL your answers in terms of the job for which you are being examined.

Basis of Rating

Probably you will forget most of these "do's" and "don'ts" when you walk into the oral interview room. Even remembering them all will not ensure you a passing grade. Perhaps you did not have the qualifications in the first place. But remembering them will help you to put your best foot forward, without treading on the toes of the board members.

Rumor and popular opinion to the contrary notwithstanding, an oral board wants you to make the best appearance possible. They know you are under pressure – but they also want to see how you respond to it as a guide to what your reaction would be under the pressures of the job you seek. They will be influenced by the degree of poise you display, the personal traits you show and the manner in which you respond.

ABOUT THIS BOOK

This book contains tests divided into Examination Sections. Go through each test, answering every question in the margin. We have also attached a sample answer sheet at the back of the book that can be removed and used. At the end of each test look at the answer key and check your answers. On the ones you got wrong, look at the right answer choice and learn. Do not fill in the answers first. Do not memorize the questions and answers, but understand the answer and principles involved. On your test, the questions will likely be different from the samples. Questions are changed and new ones added. If you understand these past questions you should have success with any changes that arise. Tests may consist of several types of questions. We have additional books on each subject should more study be advisable or necessary for you. Finally, the more you study, the better prepared you will be. This book is intended to be the last thing you study before you walk into the examination room. Prior study of relevant texts is also recommended. NLC publishes some of these in our Fundamental Series. Knowledge and good sense are important factors in passing your exam. Good luck also helps. So now study this Passbook, absorb the material contained within and take that knowledge into the examination. Then do your best to pass that exam.

EXAMINATION SECTION

EXAMINATION SECTION
TEST 1

DIRECTIONS: Each question or incomplete statement is followed by several suggested answers or completions. Select the one that BEST answers the question or completes the statement. *PRINT THE LETTER OF THE CORRECT ANSWER IN THE SPACE AT THE RIGHT.*

1. A cleaner who is new on the job did not understand an order given to him over the phone by his supervisor. He went to an experienced cleaner and asked him to explain the order to him.
   His action was

   A. *proper* because the experienced cleaner would most likely know what the supervisor meant
   B. *improper* because he should have asked the supervisor to explain the order
   C. *proper* because if he had asked the supervisor to explain the order, he would have looked stupid and also wasted the supervisor's time
   D. *improper* because he should have carried out the order to the best of his ability

2. While pouring a chemical fluid into a pail of water, a cleaner splashes some of the fluid in his eye.
   The FIRST thing he should do is wash his eye with

   A. a salve
   B. a light oil
   C. rubbing alcohol
   D. running water

3. During a rush hour, a cleaner notices a blind person with a seeing-eye dog on the subway platform. He tells the blind person that he must go up to the street and take a bus.
   His action was

   A. *proper* because a blind person should not travel by subway during rush hours
   B. *improper* because a blind person is not allowed to take a dog on the bus
   C. *proper* because many people riding the subway are frightened by dogs
   D. *improper* because a blind person with a seeing-eye dog is allowed to ride on the subway

4. A cleaner threw an oily rag into the corner of the cleaner's room, intending to leave it there until the next time he needed it.
   His action was

   A. *proper* because he could easily find it when he wanted it
   B. *improper* because it made the room look untidy
   C. *proper* because it was out of the sight of passengers
   D. *improper* because oily rags can easily catch fire

5. If a cleaner notices that any subway station light bulbs are burned out, he is required to report it immediately.
   The MAIN reason for promptly reporting this condition is to

   A. avoid complaints from passengers
   B. keep his supervisor informed
   C. prevent accidents
   D. make a good impression on his supervisor

6. Cleaners must be very careful not to let water get into escalator pits and on escalator machinery, or on the electrical components of escalators.
The MAIN reason for this precaution is that

   A. water may cause rust
   B. electrical parts do not need cleaning
   C. water and oil do not mix
   D. water may cause a short circuit

7. The MAIN reason for keeping a change booth locked at all times is to keep out

   A. noise
   B. drafts of air
   C. angry passengers
   D. thieves

Questions 8-10.

DIRECTIONS: Questions 8 through 10 are to be answered on the basis of the information contained in the following instructions on FIRST AID KITS.

FIRST AID KITS

First aid kits will be used only in case of injury to employees or passengers. A REPORT OF USE OF FIRST AID KIT form will be prepared in triplicate and forwarded to the Station Department Office whenever the seal of the kit is broken, regardless of whether any of the contents is used.

After use, the kit will be temporarily resealed with a shurlock seal bearing the impress of the booth punch. An outside tag will be attached to the seal with the following information on the back of the tag:

Opened: _____ A.M./P.M. _____
              (Time)   (Date)
By _____
      (Name)   (Title)   (Pass No.)

Resealed: _____ A.M./P.M. _____
              (Time)   (Date)
By _____
      (Name)   (Title)   (Pass No.)

Upon receipt of REPORT OF USE OF FIRST AID KIT form, the P.M. Station Supervisor will arrange to replace the items used and reseal the kit, using a special seal punch.

8. First aid kits may be used whenever

   A. the seal of the kit is broken
   B. the Station Supervisor approves
   C. their contents have to be checked
   D. there is an injury to employees or passengers

9. Who should arrange for the replacement of the items used in a first aid kit? 9.____
   The

   A. railroad clerk B. cleaner
   C. Station Supervisor D. employee who used the kit

10. The information written on the back of the tag attached to the first aid kit should contain 10.____
    the

    A. social security number of the person who opened the kit
    B. pass number of the person who resealed the kit
    C. time when the accident took place
    D. place where the accident happened

Questions 11-14.

DIRECTIONS: Questions 11 through 14 are to be answered on the basis of the information contained in the following instructions on LOST PROPERTY.

LOST PROPERTY

All inquiries for information regarding lost property will be referred to the Lost Property Office. Any Station Department employee finding a lost article, of any description, will immediately hand it over to the railroad clerk in the nearest 24-hour booth of the station where the article is found. The clerk must give the employee a receipt for the article. Should a passenger hand over a lost article to a cleaner, the cleaner will offer to escort the passenger to the nearest 24-hour booth in order that a receipt may be given by the railroad clerk there. If the passenger declines, the cleaner will accept the lost article without giving a receipt and proceed as described above. Each employee who receives lost property will be held responsible for it unless he produces a receipt for it from another employee. Should any lost property disappear, the last employee who signed for it will be held strictly accountable.

11. If a cleaner turns in a lost article to a railroad clerk in the nearest 24-hour booth, he 11.____
    should make sure that he

    A. gets a receipt for the article
    B. notifies his supervisor about the lost article
    C. finds out the name of the owner of the article
    D. writes a report on the incident

12. If a lost article disappears after a cleaner has properly turned it in to the railroad clerk in 12.____
    the nearest 24-hour booth, the one who will be held accountable is the

    A. person who found the lost article
    B. cleaner who turned in the article
    C. supervisor in charge of the station
    D. last employee to sign a receipt for the article

13. A passenger finds a lost article and gives it to a cleaner. 13.____
    The cleaner gives the passenger a receipt.
    The cleaner's action was

A. *proper* because the passenger was relieved of any responsibility for the lost article
B. *improper* because the cleaner should have offered to escort the passenger to the nearest 24-hour booth
C. *proper* because the cleaner is required to give the passenger a receipt
D. *improper* because the cleaner should have sent the passenger to the Lost Property Office

14. A cleaner finds a five-dollar bill on a crowded station platform. Three passengers who see him pick it up rush up and claim the money. The first passenger said he had just taken a roll of bills out of his pocket and must have dropped it. The second said he had just given two five-dollar bills to his wife, and she had dropped one of them. The third said he had a hole in his pocket and the bill fell out of it.
The cleaner should

   A. give the five-dollar bill to the second passenger because he had his wife as a witness
   B. give the five-dollar bill to the third passenger because he had a hole in his pocket
   C. keep the five-dollar bill
   D. bring the five-dollar bill to the railroad clerk in the nearest 24-hour booth

Questions 15-20.

DIRECTIONS: Questions 15 through 20 are to be answered on the basis of the information contained in the CLEANING REPORT below.

CLEANING REPORT

To Cleaner (TA) J. Brown Badge No. 3461 Pass No. 327351

The following cleaning report must be filled out by you and handed in before you go off duty. Part I shall be prepared by a Station Supervisor, Assistant Station Supervisor, RR Clerk or Claim Investigator. Part II must then be filled out by you.

PART I

This part must be filled in by Station Supervisor, Assistant Station Supervisor, RR Clerk, or Claim Investigator before second part is completed by Cleaner (TA).

Date of Accident Feb. 27, 1985 Time 11:30 A.M./P.M. Line A
Station 34th Street   Exact Location Stairway S-6
Name of Injured Gregory Peckham Address 124 W. 16th St., N.Y., N.Y.
Accident occurred before/while/after John Brown
Title Cleaner (TA)   Pass No. 327351 came on duty/ was on duty/went off duty

PART II

This part must be completed and all questions answered by the above Cleaner but only after Part I has been filled in.
I John Brown Pass No. 327351 was on duty at the 34th St.
Station on Feb. 27, 1985 from 8:00 A.M./P.M. to 4:00 A.M./P.M.

Upon my arrival at the station, I proceeded to inspect and then clean the entire station including Stairway S-6 and left it in good condition I swept and cleaned that part of the station at about 11:00 A.M./P.M., the same as I do on every tour of duty and cleaned and inspected it again at about 2:00 A.M./P.M. before I went off duty.
Did you inspect scene after accident? Yes If you did so, give time and condition.
Date Feb. 27, 1985 Time 11:45 A.M./P.M. Condition Clean and in good condition .
Weather Conditions Clear
Was there any snow or ice on the street surface? No
Was there any snow or ice on the part of the station involved in accident? No
Were there any defects or obstructions at place of accident? No REMARKS: (Here give details as to conditions existing and all you know about this accident.)
I saw a passenger lose his balance while descending Stairway S-6 and fall down the steps. He bruised his face. I inspected the stairway at 11:45 A.M. and found it clean and in good condition.
Did you see the accident? Yes Date report was signed by you Date report was signed by you Feb. 27, 1985
FULL NAME John Brown ADDRESS 154 E. 18th St.. N.Y.. N.Y. Apt. 3C

15. The accident occurred on

    A. Stairway N-6
    B. Northbound platform
    C. Southbound platform
    D. Stairway S-6

16. The stairway where the accident occurred was cleaned at

    A. 8:00 AM B. 11:00 AM C. 11:45 AM D. 4:00 PM

17. Part I of the Cleaning Report may be filled out by any of the following employees EXCEPT the

    A. Station Supervisor
    B. Cleaner
    C. RR Clerk
    D. Claim Investigator

18. The accident to the passenger took place at

    A. 11:00 AM B. 11:30 AM C. 11:45 AM D. 2:00 PM

19. Part II of the Cleaning Report was made out by the

    A. Assistant Station Supervisor
    B. Station Supervisor
    C. Cleaner
    D. Railroad Clerk

20. What was the pass number of the Cleaner?

    A. 323751 B. 372351 C. 327351 D. 327531

KEY (CORRECT ANSWERS)

1. B
2. D
3. D
4. D
5. C

6. D
7. D
8. D
9. C
10. B

11. A
12. D
13. B
14. D
15. D

16. B
17. B
18. B
19. C
20. C

———

TEST 2

DIRECTIONS: Each question or incomplete statement is followed by several suggested answers or completions. Select the one that BEST answers the question or completes the statement. *PRINT THE LETTER OF THE CORRECT ANSWER IN THE SPACE AT THE RIGHT.*

Questions 1-7.

DIRECTIONS: Questions 1 through 7 are to be answered on the basis of the information given in the following description of MAJOR DUTIES.

MAJOR DUTIES

SWEEPING:
To be done with pre-dampened sawdust.

CLEANING BOOTHS:
Wash all interior and exterior walls and windows. Sweep, scrub, and mop floors inside of the booth and the three-foot area around the outside of the booth. Clean and polish all metal inside and outside of booth and in control areas. Dust and remove all debris from top of booth. Dust all railings and turnstiles in control area. Scrub and mop floor area under and around turnstiles and exit gates.

CLEANING TOILETS:
Wash and disinfect all walls, ceilings, doors, and modesty shields. Scrub, disinfect, and mop floors. Scrub and disinfect all bowls, basins, and urinals. Remove all debris and dust all shelves, ledges, and lockers. Apply a light coat of lemon oil to all painted and slateback surfaces.

CLEAN ESCALATOR:
All surfaces are cleaned by dusting. In the case of spillage (soda, beer, etc.), a clean rag will be dipped in a light soap solution and excessive water removed. Area should be thoroughly dried so as to prevent streaking.

CANISTERS AND SOLAR CANS:
Remove bags or wheeled inserts. Sweep out interior, then scrub and disinfect inside and the three-foot area around the unit being cleaned.

BENCHES:
Should be scrubbed and disinfected as well as dried. Duties also include the three-foot adjacent area.

CLEANING TILES AND GUTTERS:
Includes washing and rinsing of tile areas using soap and water solutions applied with a Tampico brush and rinsed with clean water and using a rinse brush. Gutters are cleaned by scrubbing and rinsing with a Palmyra brush dipped in a soap, disinfectant, and water solution. Rinsing is done with clean water.

CLEANING COLUMNS AND SIGNS:
Includes scrubbing and rinsing of all columns and signs, as well as adjacent floor areas.

2 (#2)

1. Pre-dampened sawdust is used for   1._____

    A. scrapping   B. disinfecting
    C. cleaning tiles   D. sweeping

2. A Tampico brush is used for washing   2._____

    A. tile areas   B. toilets
    C. basins   D. booths

3. A cleaner must clean a 3-foot area around a(n)   3._____

    A. escalator   B. booth   C. post light   D. gutter

4. Gutters should be cleaned by   4._____

    A. scrubbing and rinsing   B. scraping and washing
    C. dusting and oiling   D. polishing and drying

5. Of the following, the object which should be cleaned by dusting is a(n)   5._____

    A. bowl   B. solar can   C. escalator   D. urinal

6. A light coat of lemon oil should be applied to   6._____

    A. painted surfaces   B. floors
    C. escalators   D. turnstiles

7. A cleaner should remove bags before cleaning   7._____

    A. benches   B. solar cans
    C. booths   D. turnstiles

Questions 8-14.

DIRECTIONS: Questions 8 through 14 are to be answered on the basis of the information given in the following SCHEDULED DUTIES of the cleaner assigned to JOB 169.

SCHEDULED DUTIES

<u>JOB 169</u>	WEST 4TH STREET -- *A* LINE 8:00 AM - 4:00 PM -- MONDAY <u>TO FRIDAY ONLY BOOTH CLOSED SATURDAY AND SUNDAY</u>
8:00 AM	REPORT ON DUTY IN UNIFORM TO BOOTH N-83 -W.4TH STREET
8:00 AM - 8:30 AM	Turn off Post Lights at N-83 area. Clean and disinfect crew toilets South end of Northbound lower platform. Fill paper dispensers.
8:30 AM - 11:00 AM	Sweep all street stairways N-83 area. Sweep all stairways leading to middle mezzanine. Scrap Northbound upper and lower platforms and North half of middle mezzanine.
11:00 AM - 11:30 AM	LUNCH -- REPORT OUT AND IN AT BOOTH N-83

11:30 AM - 2:00 PM MONDAY	**MAJOR DUTIES AT W. 4TH STREET** Sawdust sweep Southbound upper platform and passageways to and including N-81 and N-83 mezzanine.
TUESDAY	Sawdust sweep Southbound lower platform and all stairways leading to it.
WEDNESDAY	Sawdust sweep 1/2 mezzanine from center to South end.
THURSDAY	Sawdust sweep 1/2 mezzanine from center to North end.
FRIDAY	Sawdust sweep Northbound upper platform and passageways to and including N-80 and N-83 mezzanine.
2:00 PM - 2:30 PM	Disinfect urine areas behind North end stairways and N-81 area.
2:30 PM - 4:00 PM	Rescrap entire area as covered above. Turn on Post Lights before going off duty.
4:00 PM	REPORT OFF DUTY AT BOOTH N-83 - W. 4TH STREET

8. The cleaner assigned to JOB 169 should turn off the Post Lights between _____ and _____.

    A. 3:30 PM; 4:00 PM
    B. 2:30 PM; 3:00 PM
    C. 8:00 AM; 8:30 AM
    D. 10:30 AM; 11:00 AM

    8.____

9. The cleaner should sawdust sweep 1/2 mezzanine from center to North end on

    A. Mondays
    B. Tuesdays
    C. Wednesdays
    D. Thursdays

    9.____

10. The cleaner should sweep all stairways leading to the middle mezzanine in the N-83 area between _____ and _____.

    A. 8:00 AM; 8:30 AM
    B. 8:30 AM; 11:00 AM
    C. 11:30 AM; 2:00 PM
    D. 2:30 PM; 4:00 PM

    10.____

11. The cleaner should report off duty at Booth

    A. N-83   B. N-81   C. N-80   D. S-83

    11.____

12. Each day, the cleaner should clean and disinfect the crew toilets at the _____ end of the _____ platform.

    A. South; Northbound lower
    B. South; Southbound lower
    C. North; Northbound upper
    D. South; Northbound upper

    12.____

13. A MAJOR duty of JOB 169 on Friday is to sawdust sweep

    A. Southbound lower platform
    B. Northbound upper platform
    C. Southbound upper platform
    D. 1/2 mezzanine from center to South end

    13.____

14. Which of the following is a MAJOR duty of JOB 169 to be performed between 11:30 AM and 2:00 PM?

    A. Sweep all stairways in the N-83 area
    B. Sawdust sweep all stairways leading to Southbound lower platform
    C. Disinfect urine areas behind North end stairways
    D. Fill paper dispensers in crew toilets

Questions 15-20.

DIRECTIONS: Questions 15 through 20 are to be answered on the basis of the information contained in the following instructions on SWEEPING.

SWEEPING

All sweeping must be done with damp sawdust, which is used to prevent the raising of dust when sweeping platforms and mezzanines. Soak sawdust thoroughly in a bucket of water for two to three hours before use. Drain before use so that no stains are left on concrete from excess water. In order to keep sawdust moist while being used, spread for an area of 120 feet in advance of actual sweeping. Never sweep sawdust over drains. To assure good footing, do not spread it on stairways or on damp or wet floor areas.

15. Dampened sawdust should be used when

    A. scrapping   B. dusting
    C. sweeping   D. mopping

16. Of the following procedures, which is the CORRECT order to be followed when sweeping with sawdust?
    _____ the sawdust.

    A. Soak, drain, and spread   B. Spread, drain, and soak
    C. Spread, soak, and drain   D. Drain, spread, and soak

17. Of the following, it is MOST correct to soak the sawdust in a bucket of water for _____ hour(s).

    A. a half-hour to an   B. one to two
    C. two to three   D. three to four

18. The water should be drained from the bucket of sawdust so that excess water does NOT

    A. cause passengers to lose their footing
    B. stain the concrete
    C. flood the tracks
    D. slow down the sweeping

19. Sawdust is dampened in order to

    A. assure good footing on stairways
    B. prevent the raising of dust when sweeping
    C. prevent the staining of concrete
    D. cool off platforms

20. The dampened sawdust may be spread on 20.____

    A. wet floors   B. drains
    C. stairways   D. mezzanines

KEY (CORRECT ANSWERS)

1. D	11. A
2. A	12. A
3. B	13. B
4. A	14. B
5. C	15. C
6. A	16. A
7. B	17. C
8. C	18. B
9. D	19. B
10. B	20. D

TEST 3

DIRECTIONS: Each question or incomplete statement is followed by several suggested answers or completions. Select the one that BEST answers the question or completes the statement. *PRINT THE LETTER OF THE CORRECT ANSWER IN THE SPACE AT THE RIGHT.*

1. The BEST way to store a sweeping brush when it is not in use is to 1.___

   A. rest the brush on the floor, handle up
   B. rest the brush on the floor, handle down
   C. hang the brush on pegs or nails
   D. stack the brush with other brushes, one on top of the other

2. The word *graffiti* refers to 2.___

   A. markings on walls
   B. dirt on platform
   C. garbage on stairways
   D. advertising on trains

3. Disinfectant is used to 3.___

   A. dissolve grease
   B. melt ice
   C. kill germs
   D. soften water

4. Detergent is used to 4.___

   A. wax floors
   B. bale refuse
   C. clean sinks
   D. polish metal

5. Deodorant is used to 5.___

   A. wash tile walls
   B. dampen sawdust
   C. dust furniture
   D. drive away unpleasant odors

Questions 6-12.

DIRECTIONS: Cleaners in the Station Department are sometimes assigned as lunch or comfort reliefs for booth clerks. Questions 6 through 12 are concerned with making change. A fare is to be considered as worth $2.50.

6. If a passenger gives you 14 quarters, 12 dimes and 6 nickels, how many fares should you give him? 6.___

   A. 1   B. 2   C. 3   D. 4

7. How much should a passenger pay for 3 fares? 7.___

   A. $2.50   B. $3.50   C. $5.00   D. $7.50

8. If a passenger gives you a $20 bill and asks for 6 fares, how much change should you give him? 8.___

   A. $2.50   B. $3.50   C. $5.00   D. $7.50

9. If a passenger gives you a ten-dollar bill and asks you to give him as many fares as possible, how many should you give him?

   A. 2 B. 3 C. 4 D. 5

10. If a passenger gives you a $50 bill and asks for 5 fares, how much change should you give him?

    A. $37.50 B. $32.50 C. $25.00 D. $20.00

11. If a passenger gives you 8 one-dollar bills and asks for 5 fares, you should ask him for an additional

    A. $4.50 B. $4.00 C. $3.50 D. $2.50

12. If a passenger gives you 7 quarters, 5 dimes, and 9 nickels, how many fares should you give him?

    A. 0 B. 1 C. 2 D. 3

13. Grand Central Station is located in Manhattan at

    A. 34th Street and 7th Ave.
    B. Union Square
    C. Columbus Circle
    D. 42nd Street and Vanderbilt Ave.

14. Citi Field is located in

    A. Manhattan
    B. The Bronx
    C. Brooklyn
    D. Queens

15. The Empire State Building is located in Manhattan at

    A. Lenox Avenue and 125th Street
    B. Broadway and 42nd Street
    C. Fifth Avenue and 34th Street
    D. West 4th Street and Broadway

16. If a passenger asks you how to get to the Statue of Liberty, you should direct him to

    A. South Ferry
    B. the Verrazano Bridge
    C. the Port Authority Bus Terminal
    D. Penn Station

17. Lincoln Center for the Performing Arts is located in Manhattan at

    A. Broadway and 64th Street
    B. Central Park West and 86th Street
    C. Wall Street and Broadway
    D. 6th Avenue and 50th Street

18. City Hall is located NEAREST to

    A. South Ferry
    B. the Brooklyn Bridge
    C. Union Square
    D. Greenwich Village

19. The World Trade Center was located in
    A. The Bronx   B. Brooklyn
    C. Manhattan   D. Queens

20. Madison Square Garden is located
    A. in Central Park   B. at Penn Station
    C. near Borough Hall   D. at Coney Island

KEY (CORRECT ANSWERS)

1.	C	11.	A
2.	A	12.	B
3.	C	13.	D
4.	C	14.	D
5.	D	15.	C
6.	B	16.	A
7.	D	17.	A
8.	C	18.	B
9.	C	19.	C
10.	A	20.	B

EXAMINATION SECTION
TEST 1

DIRECTIONS: Each question or incomplete statement is followed by several suggested answers or completions. Select the one that BEST answers the question or completes the statement. *PRINT THE LETTER OF THE CORRECT ANSWER IN THE SPACE AT THE RIGHT.*

1. Assume that you are assigned responsibility for the car body painting in one of the main car shops and you are advised that the exterior painting on recently painted cars from this shop is unsatisfactory. Upon inspecting the cars in question, you find that the paint finish shows an excessive amount of sagging and running.
   The following painting practices are offered for your consideration as having been possible causes of the runs and sags in the painted finish:
   I. Too much thinner was used.
   II. Too little drying time was allowed between coats.
   III. The spray gun was held too close to the surface of the work.
   IV. The spray gun was held too far away from the surface of the work.
   V. The air pressure used in the spray gun was too low.
   VI. The air pressure used in the spray gun was too high.
   VII. The spray gun was moved too rapidly over the work surface.
   Which of the following suggested answers CORRECTLY lists the possible causes of the runs and sags in the painted finish?

   A. I and IV
   B. IV *only*
   C. I, II, III, V
   D. VI and VII

1.____

2. A foreman has been training a group of newly appointed maintainers in the proper techniques for spray-painting car bodies. Assume that you have been observing these maintainers as they work in order to evaluate how well they have learned to use the spray equipment.
   The following practices are offered for your consideration as possibly being indicative of proper spray painting:
   A maintainer
   I. swings the spray gun in an arc formed by rotating his body from the hips while holding the spray gun
   II. makes his strokes by moving the spray gun parallel to the surface of the work
   III. holds his gun at right angles to the surface of the work
   IV. keeps a constant 20-inch distance between the gun nozzle and the surface of the work
   V. starts each new stroke underneath the previous stroke so that the edge of each stroke touches only the edge of the preceding stroke
   Which of the following suggested answers CORRECTLY lists the practices indicative of proper spray painting?

   A. I *only*
   B. II and III
   C. III and IV
   D. I, II, III, IV

2.____

3. Assume that you are assigned to supervise a welding shop. The following practices are offered for your consideration as possibly appropriate to shop safety in the handling of gas cylinders.
   I. Keep all unused spare pressurized gas cylinders resting on their side in a suitable rack
   II. Provide a manifold for the purpose of centralizing a continuous acetylene supply
   III. Coat the threads on the regulator valve with a light grease when installing it on the cylinder
   IV. Keep the valve protecting caps on the gas cylinder while not in use

   Which of the following suggested answers CORRECTLY lists *unsafe* statements regarding the usage of gas cylinders?

   A. I and III
   B. II and IV
   C. III and IV
   D. I, II, III, IV

4. In the car maintenance department, a five-step management process is suggested for the solution of problems.
   The steps consist of: planning, organizing, controlling, executing, and

   A. achieving
   B. adapting
   C. adjusting
   D. appraising

5. The traction motors for subway cars are of the series type; that is, the motor armature and field are connected in series.
   The following statements of the characteristics of various types of motors are to be reviewed to select those characteristics that are appropriate to series type motors used in subway trains.
   I. Develops a high starting torque
   II. Direction of rotation can be reversed by interchanging the connections of the motor field
   III. Direction of rotation can be reversed by placing the armature and field in parallel
   IV. Speed can be increased by shunting the motor field winding with resistance
   V. Speed can be increased by applying full rail voltage to each motor on the truck

   Which of the following suggested answers lists CORRECT statements of the characteristics of the series type motor which make it appropriate for propelling subway trains?

   A. I *only*
   B. I and II
   C. I, II, IV
   D. I, II, III, IV, V

6. The Woodward height adjuster on a car truck is used to compensate PRIMARILY for

   A. load sensor valve malfunction
   B. wheel wear
   C. journal bearing wear
   D. traction motor pinion and gear misalignment

7. When a conference or a group discussion is tending to turn into a *bull session* without constructive purpose, the BEST action to take is to

   A. reprimand the leader of the *bull session*
   B. redirect the discussion to the business at hand
   C. dismiss the meeting and reschedule it for another day
   D. allow the *bull session* to continue

7.____

8. Assume that you have been assigned responsibility for the overhaul program of the master controller on the R-32 cars in which a high production rate is mandatory. From past experience, you know that your foremen do not perform equally well in the various types of jobs given to them. Which of the following methods should you use in selecting foremen for the specific types of work involved in the overhaul program?

   A. Leave the method of selecting foremen to your supervisor
   B. Assign each foreman to the work he does best
   C. Allow each foreman to choose his own job
   D. Assign each foreman to a job which will permit him to improve his own abilities

8.____

9. Which one of the following is the PRIMARY objective in drawing up a set of specifications for materials to be purchased?

   A. Establishment of standard sizes
   B. Outline of intended use
   C. Method of inspection
   D. Control of quality

9.____

10. In the subway system, a major distinction between the cars of the A Division and of the B Division is that the _____ Division cars _____.

    A. B; cannot operate on the A Division
    B. A; cannot operate on the B Division
    C. B; are shorter than the A Division cars
    D. A; are higher than the B Division cars

10.____

11. Of the following, the MOST important function of an assistant supervisor is to

    A. write pertinent reports to his supervisor
    B. answer technical questions from his foremen
    C. delegate critical responsibilities to his foremen
    D. supervise in an efficient manner

11.____

12. Assume that you have determined that the work of one of your foremen and the men he supervises is consistently behind schedule. When you discuss this situation with the foreman, he tells you that his men are poor workers and then complains that he must spend all of his time checking on their work.
    The following actions are offered for your consideration as possible ways of solving the problem of poor performance of the foreman and his men:
    I. Review the work standards with the foreman and determine whether they are reliable
    II. Tell the foreman that you will recommend him for the foreman's training course for retraining

12.____

III. Ask the foreman for the names of the maintainers and then replace them as soon as possible
IV. Tell the foreman that you expect him to meet a satisfactory level of performance
V. Tell the foreman to insist that his men work overtime to catch up to the schedule
VI. Tell the foreman to review the type and amount of training he has given the maintainers
VII. Tell the foreman that he will be out of a job if he does not produce on schedule
VIII. Avoid all criticism of the foreman and his methods

Which of the following suggested answers CORRECTLY lists the proper actions to be taken to solve the problem of poor performance of the foreman and his men?

A. I, II, IV, VI
B. I, III, V, VII
C. II, III, VI, VIII
D. IV, V, VI, VIII

13. Assume that one of the foremen in a training course, which you are conducting, proposes a poor solution for a maintenance problem.
Of the following, the BEST course of action for you to take is to

A. accept the solution tentatively, and correct it during the next class meeting
B. point out all the defects of this proposed solution and wait until somebody thinks of a better solution
C. try to get the class to reject this proposed solution and develop a better solution
D. let the matter pass since somebody will present a better solution as the class work proceeds

14. While making a walking tour of the wheel shop, you observe a maintainer who is operating a hoisting system, replacing a sling which will be used to lift heavily laden pallets. The new sling which will now be used is identical to the old sling in construction except that the wire ropes are longer. The maintainer finds that the angle which the legs of the sling make with the horizontal changed from 45° on the old sling to 60° on the new sling. The following are possible changes in capability of the hoisting system directly resulting from the new sling.
The following are possible changes in capability of the hoisting system directly resulting from the new sling.
   I. The load carrying capability of the sling has been increased.
   II. The load carrying capability of the overhead hoist has been increased.
   III. The load carrying capability of the sling has been decreased.
   IV. The maximum clearance between the pallet and the shop floor has been decreased.

Which of the following suggested answers CORRECTLY describes the changes in the capability of the hoisting system directly resulting from the increased angle of the legs of the sling with the horizontal?

A. I, II
B. III only
C. I, IV
D. I, II, IV

15. In the R-44 car, the dynamic brake feedback sends a signal to a particular unit which eliminates the pneumatic brake operation until the speed of the train is approximately 10 MPH or less.
    The name of this unit is

    A. GR-90 tread brake unit
    B. A-13 electronic operating unit
    C. G-4B pneumatic operating unit
    D. J-relay valve

16. In statistical reports on shop injuries, the expression which describes a work injury resulting in death, permanent total disability, permanent partial disability, or temporary total disability is a

    A. medical treatment injury
    B. disabling injury
    C. disabling injury severity rate
    D. disabling injury frequency rate

17. The MAJOR components in the R-44 car RT 5C brake equipment are the _____ compressor, A-13 electronic unit, _____ pneumatic unit, and _____ brake unit.

    A. D-3; G4B; GR-90
    B. D-3; G4B; ME-23
    C. A-1; G4B; GR-90
    D. A-1; J; GR-90

18. In the R-44 car, an A-13 electronic operating unit is used to convert increasing or decreasing current level in the P-wire to an electrical request to the pneumatic operating unit for decreasing or increasing the brake cylinder pressure.
    The condition that must exist to terminate the change in pressure in the brake cylinder is that the feedback signal from the

    A. dynamic brake request is 1 milliamp (DC) less than the P-wire request
    B. dynamic brake request matches the P-wire request
    C. pneumatic operating unit matches the P-wire request
    D. pneumatic operating unit is 1 milliamp (DC) more than the P-wire request

Questions 19-21.

DIRECTIONS: When answering Questions 19 through 21, refer to the ACCIDENT CODE CLASSIFICATION listed below. The code lists letters that identify the responsibility for an accident and numbers that identify the cause of an accident. In answering the questions, select both the appropriate letter and number that classifies the accident described in the question, such as A-1, B-2, etc.

ACCIDENT CODE CLASSIFICATION

Responsibility

A. Supervision

B. Employee

C. Other Employee

D. Impractical to control

E. Control of other than company or employee

Cause of Accident

1. Poor housekeeping
2. Defective construction, equipment, design
3. Tools, equipment (improper use or handling)
4. Protective equipment not provided
5. Protective equipment not used
6. Improper or inadequate instructions
7. Inattention
8. Failure to observe rules or orders

19. A maintainer suffers an eye injury while drilling holes in a casting. Investigation revealed that he was not wearing the approved type of safety glasses.
    The classification for this injury should be

    A. A-4   B. A-6   C. B-4   D. B-5

20. A maintainer working near an open pit normally equipped with a removable guard rail falls into the pit and suffers head wounds.
    The classification for this accident should be

    A. A-4   B. A-7   C. B-4   D. B-7

21. A maintainer working at his regular station suffers eye burns as a result of welding work being done on an air tank located about 10 feet from the maintainer's work station.
    The classification of this injury should be

    A. A-2   B. A-4   C. B-5   D. B-7

22. It has been found necessary to remove a component from a printed circuit card used on an R-44 car.
    Before the component can be removed, it is NECESSARY to

    A. remove the plastic coating from the card
    B. clean the card in an ultrasonic cleaning bath
    C. unsolder the multi-pin connector
    D. connect all capacitors on the card to a common ground

23. Of the following, the statement concerning hydraulic lifting jacks which is MOST appropriate is that, in general, the working fluid will

    A. not increase in temperature when loaded
    B. not change its viscosity when loaded
    C. increase in volume when loaded
    D. not freeze at a temperature of 32 °F

23.____

24. A car wheel should be pressed on a truck axle with a force that is between _____ and _____ tons.

    A. 24; 38   B. 42; 53   C. 68; 90   D. 100; 142

24.____

25. The reporting card which should be used for recording the serial number of an air compressor installed on a subway car during overhaul is the

    A. individual car case history report
    B. road car inspector report
    C. R-10 and up cars-inspection card
    D. repair card, car level

25.____

KEY (CORRECT ANSWERS)

1.	C	11.	D
2.	B	12.	A
3.	A	13.	C
4.	D	14.	C
5.	C	15.	B
6.	B	16.	B
7.	B	17.	A
8.	B	18.	C
9.	D	19.	D
10.	A	20.	D

21. B
22. A
23. D
24. C
25. D

TEST 2

DIRECTIONS: Each question or incomplete statement is followed by several suggested answers or completions. Select the one that BEST answers the question or completes the statement. *PRINT THE LETTER OF THE CORRECT ANSWER IN THE SPACE AT THE RIGHT.*

1. The maintenance of subway cars is a continuing process. As a supervisor, you should be seeking ways to improve the efficiency of shop operations by means such as changing established work procedures.
   The following are offered as possible actions that you should consider in changing established work procedures.
   I. Make changes only when your foremen agree to them
   II. Discuss changes with your supervisor before putting them into practice
   III. Standardize any operation which is performed on a continuing basis
   IV. Make changes quickly and quietly in order to avoid dissent
   V. Secure expert guidance before instituting unfamiliar procedures
   Of the following suggested answers, the one that describes the actions to be taken to change established work procedures is

   A. I, IV, V   B. II, III, V
   C. III, IV, V   D. I, II, III, IV, V

   1.____

2. If a pair of channels are to be welded together to form a built-up beam, the arrangement which will produce the greatest transverse load carrying capacity is shown by the following cross section:

   2.____

   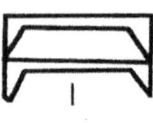
   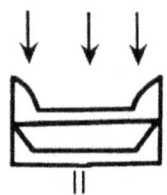
   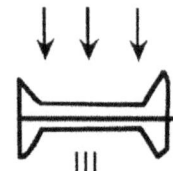
   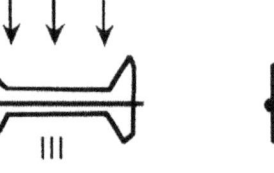

   A. I   B. II   C. III   D. IV

3. The CHIEF advantage of a differential chain hoist over an ordinary block and tackle is that

   A. a load suspended from a chain hoist will remain stationary without attention
   B. heavier loads can be lifted with a chain hoist than with a block and tackle
   C. loads can be raised more rapidly with a chain hoist than with a block and tackle
   D. the chain hoist costs less than the block and tackle

   3.____

4. In a work gang using a power hoist lift, it is the generally accepted practice that only one man in the group gives the signals to the operator of the hoist. There is, however, one exception.
   In this exception, any one of the group is permitted to give the _____ signal.

   A. boom-up   B. hoist   C. swing   D. stop

   4.____

5. A supervisor determined that a foreman, without informing his superior, delegated responsibility for checking time cards to a member of his gang. The supervisor then called the foreman into his office where he reprimanded the foreman.
This action of the supervisor in reprimanding the foreman was

   A. *proper,* because the checking of time cards is the foreman's responsibility and should not be delegated
   B. *proper,* because the foreman did not ask the supervisor for permission to delegate responsibility
   C. *improper,* because the foreman may no longer take the initiative in solving future problems
   D. *improper,* because the supervisor is interfering in a function which is not his responsibility

6. After completing the silver brazing of a joint with an oxyacetylene torch, the maintainer should remove the residual flux and oxide by

   A. dipping the joint in hot oil
   B. washing the joint with hot water
   C. dipping the joint in sulphuric acid
   D. grinding the joint

7. The air-conditioning system on the R-42 subway cars can be described as having

   A. two independent refrigeration units, each of 9-ton capacity
   B. one refrigeration unit of 18-ton capacity
   C. two independent refrigeration units, each of 15-ton capacity
   D. one refrigeration unit of 30-ton capacity

8. When using an oxyacetylene torch to cut steel, the flame should contain

   A. an excess amount of acetylene
   B. an excess amount of oxygen
   C. equal amounts of acetylene and oxygen
   D. only acetylene

Questions 9-11.

DIRECTIONS: The following Questions 9 through 11, inclusive, refer to the information contained in the equipment code book of the cars and shop department. In this book, car equipment defects are identified with code numbers.

9. The code number that identifies the defect of *low refrigerant* in the air conditioning system is

   A. 180   B. 198   C. 209   D. 308

10. The code number that identifies the defect in a car with a flat spot $1\frac{1}{2}$ to $2\frac{1}{2}$ inches long is

   A. 100   B. 181   C. 199   D. 213

11. The code number indicating that no defect was found on the reported *low air pressure* on a trouble car is

    A. 011   B. 041   C. 136   D. 168

12. The master controller should NOT be held in the *switching* position for a prolonged period of time because, if held in this position, the

    A. compressed air needed for braking may be wasted
    B. air brakes may be automatically actuated
    C. starting resistors may burn out
    D. train may accelerate too rapidly

13. Of the following, the conditions which BEST describe the possible causes of an emergency brake application are a(n)

    A. open conductor's valve, a brake handle in *emergency,* or a blown compressor fuse
    B. brake handle in *emergency,* a blown compressor fuse, or a broken brake pipe
    C. blown compressor fuse, a broken brake pipe, or an open conductor's valve
    D. broken brake pipe, an open conductor's valve, or a brake handle in *emergency*

14. Which of the following fuses should a maintainer remove *before* he attempts to adjust the clearance between the pendulum contacts on the electric self-lapping portion of the ME 42B and ME 43 brake valves?

    A. ME 2   B. L 2   C. P 2   D. B 2

15. A road car inspector reports that the motorman's indication is dim.
Of the following, the *probable* cause is that the

    A. batteries are weak
    B. air pressure is too high
    C. third rail voltage is too low
    D. air pressure is too low

16. Two yellow lanterns adjacent to the track indicate that

    A. a train is stalled
    B. men are working on the tracks
    C. a section of the subway is flooded
    D. power has been removed from a section of the third rail

17. The transit authority uses General Motors diesel engines on the crane cars.
The starting of this engine by a maintainer with liquid fuel oil in the combustion chamber is considered

    A. *good* practice, because it makes starting easier
    B. *good* practice, because it decreases fuel oil consumption rate
    C. *poor* practice, because it increases fuel oil consumption rate
    D. *poor* practice, because it could cause physical damage to the engine

18. A maintainer earns $18.66 per hour, and time and one-half for overtime over 40 hours. Each week, 15 percent of his total salary is deducted for social security and taxes. Also, each week a $27.00 deduction is made for a savings bond, and a $13.50 deduction is made for a charitable organization.
If he works a total of 46 hours in a week, his take-home pay for that week is

   A. $914.34   B. $777.15   C. $736.68   D. $616.05

19. A one-inch steel plate shown in the sketch at the right is to be used as part of a steel weldment. The weight of this plate is MOST NEARLY _____ pounds.

   A. 2,820
   B. 5,760
   C. 23,700
   D. 34,000

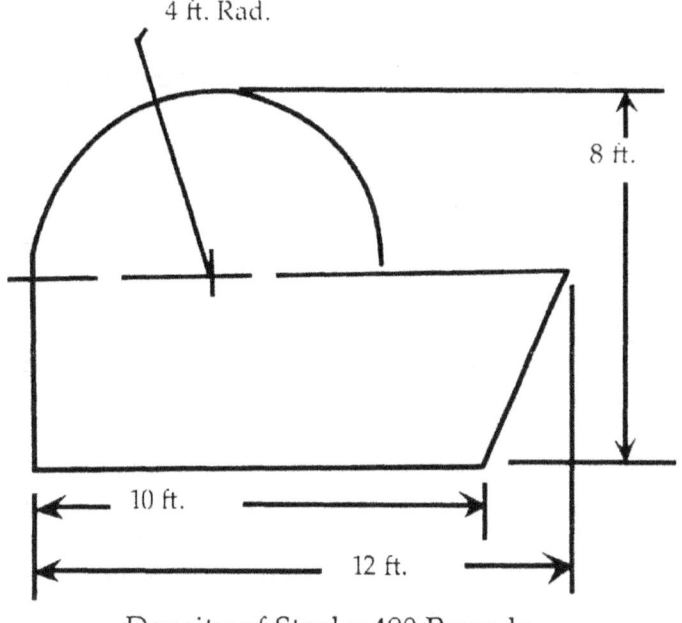

Density of Steel = 490 Pounds per Cu. Ft.

20. The refrigerant used in the R-42 air conditioning system is

   A. sulphur dioxide   B. Refrigerant-12
   C. Refrigerant-22   D. ammonia

21. In the R-44 subway car, the condensers of the air conditioning system are mounted

   A. under the car
   B. in a vertical cabinet at the No. 1 end of the A car
   C. in a false ceiling at the No. 1 end of each car
   D. in a false ceiling at the No. 2 end of each car

22. In a compression type air conditioning system, the refrigerant absorbs heat from the circulating air in the

   A. compressor   B. condenser
   C. evaporator   D. expansion valve

23. In the R-42 air conditioning system, non-cleanable type strainers are installed in the refrigerant liquid line in front of the evaporator.
To replace the strainers, it is NECESSARY to transfer the refrigerant charge to the

   A. compressor sump   B. evaporator
   C. condenser   D. receiver

24. The SMEE brake equipment uses a 3-YC air compressor which has two stages of compression.
    Air is admitted into the *first* stage by the action of the

    A. compressor camshaft opening the intake poppet valves
    B. compressor crankshaft opening the intake valves
    C. second stage discharge pressure opening the intake disc valves
    D. partial vacuum created by the downward stroke of the first stage piston opening the intake disc valves

25. Which of the following symbols should you expect to find on a circuit diagram of a printed circuit card?

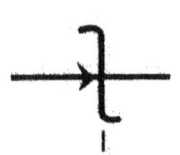 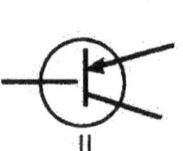 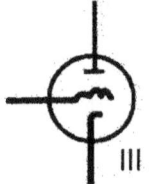 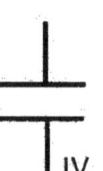

I II III IV

A. I *only*
B. I, III
C. I, II, IV
D. I, II, III, IV

KEY (CORRECT ANSWERS)

1. B		11. A	
2. D		12. C	
3. A		13. D	
4. D		14. D	
5. A		15. A	
6. B		16. B	
7. A		17. D	
8. B		18. C	
9. D		19. A	
10. B		20. C	

21. A
22. C
23. D
24. D
25. C

TEST 3

DIRECTIONS: Each question or incomplete statement is followed by several suggested answers or completions. Select the one that BEST answers the question or completes the statement. *PRINT THE LETTER OF THE CORRECT ANSWER IN THE SPACE AT THE RIGHT.*

1. An *inshot valve* is used on subway cars furnished with the SMEE brake equipment. The following statements are offered for your consideration as possibly applying to the *inshot valve*.
   It

   I. provides sufficient air to the brake cylinders to place the brake shoes against the car wheels while the dynamic brake is applied
   II. provides sufficient air to the brake cylinders to place the brake shoes against the car wheels while the pneumatic brake is applied
   III. supplies supplementary air to the brakes when the car loading requires braking effort in excess of the dynamic brake capacity
   IV. supplies control air to regulate the operation of the variable load valves

   Of the following suggested answers, the one which applies to the *inshot valve* is

   A. I only B. II only C. I, III D. I, IV

1.____

2. A supervisor while walking through the shop notices a maintainer soldering a transistor to a printed circuit card with a 150-watt soldering iron.
   This is a

   A. *good* practice, because it increases production
   B. *good* practice, because it will make a strong joint of high conductivity
   C. *poor* practice, because it may decrease the insulation resistance of the card
   D. *poor* practice, because it may damage the transistor

2.____

3. An R-44 car is brought into the shop with the complaint that the *brake pipe fails to charge*.
   The following items are offered for your consideration as causes of this reported defect.

   I. Defective recharge magnet valve
   II. Brake pipe rupture on the car body
   III. Brake pipe rupture at the draw bar
   IV. Brake pipe rupture on the head operating car

   Of the following suggested answers, the one which describes the CAUSE of the reported defect is

   A. I only   B. I, II
   C. I, II, III   D. I, II, III, IV

3.____

27

Questions 4-9.

DIRECTIONS: Questions 4 through 9 are based on the drawing of the SPINDLE SHAFT shown below. Consult this drawing when answering these questions.

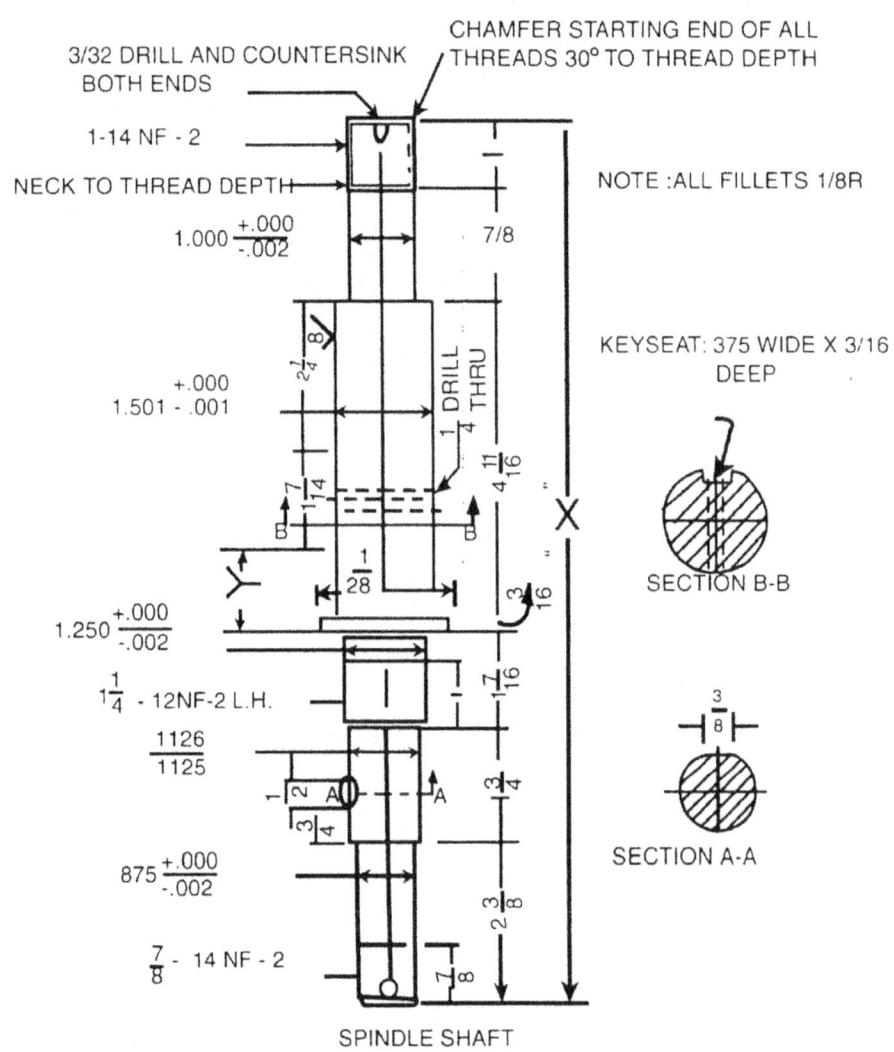

SPINDLE SHAFT

Material - Nickel - Chrome Steel 4140
Brinnell - 290
All dimensions in inches
Machine finish  all over except as noted

4. The dimensions of the steel stock from which the shaft would *probably* be machined are _____ dia. x _____ lg.

   A. $1\frac{1}{2}$"; 13" B. 2"; 14" C. $2\frac{1}{4}$"; 14" D. $2\frac{1}{2}$"; 13"

5. The number 14 in the expression 7/8-14NF-2 represents the

   A. outside diameter in millimeters
   B. pitch diameter in millimeters
   C. number of threads per inch
   D. surface roughness in microinches

6. A bronze sleeve having an I.D. of .998-.996" is to be shrunk onto the 1.000" .998" diameter portion of the shaft.
   The MAXIMUM interference between sleeve and shaft is

   A. .001"   B. .002"   C. .003"   D. .004"

7. The machine tool that would *probably* be used to obtain
   1.501 +.000/.001 diameter of the shaft is a

   A. shaper   B. planer
   C. lathe   D. cutting machine

8. The expression *Brinell-290"* indicates the

   A. type of steel used
   B. hardness of the steel
   C. tensile strength of the material
   D. density of the material

9. The *nominal* size of the square key that should be used with this shaft is _____ inch.

   A. 3/16   B. 3/8   C. 1/2   D. 1 7/16

10. In the car maintenance department, the function of analyzing and reporting train trouble is a responsibility of the _____ section.

    A. operations
    B. quality control
    C. maintenance, planning, and engineering
    D. material control

11. In the car maintenance department, the function of determining car problem areas and of developing associated corrective actions is a responsibility of the

    A. operations section
    B. quality control section
    C. maintenance, planning, and engineering section
    D. repair shop

12. The transit authority has conducted studies on the performance of fluorescent tube lights in subway cars. One of the factors studied was the effect of power interruptions caused by the contact shoes going over the third rail gaps. The following possible effects resulting from power interruptions are offered for your consideration.
    The
      I.   life of tube lights is increased
      II. life of tube lights is decreased
      III. brightness of tube lights is doubled
      IV. brightness of tube lights is increased for short intervals of time
    Of the following suggested answers, the one which describes the effects resulting from power interruptions is

    A. I *only*   B. II *only*   C. II, III   D. I, IV

13. The R-44 car has two types of circuit breakers, designated as the high voltage and the low voltage circuit breakers. On the *B* car, the low voltage circuit breakers are located at the No. 1 end of the *B* side of the car and the high voltage circuit breakers are located at the _____ side(s) of the car.

    A. No. 2 end of the *A*
    B. No. 2 end of the *B*
    C. No. 1 end on the *A*
    D. No. 1 end on both the *A* and *B*

14. A car should be stopped if the flange thickness of a wheel on this car as determined with a No. 230 gage is equal to or _____ than _____ inch(es).

    A. more; $1\frac{1}{4}$
    B. more; 1 1/8
    C. more; 1
    D. less; 15/16

15. A supervisor is informed that a truck cannot be released if the wheels on a truck-axle assembly of the truck differ by 1/8" or more in diameter.
    If the circumference of one wheel on a truck assembly which is used as a reference wheel measures 97 3/4 inches, then the *limiting* dimensions of the other wheel circumference are _____ to _____ inches.

    A. 97 1/64; 97 41/64
    B. 97 17/64; 97 57/64
    C. 97 23/64; 98 9/64
    D. 97 39/64; 98 25/64

16. The office of the superintendent of transportation must be notified when a group of maintainers is scheduled to work under flagging protection at a given track location. The notification is NECESSARY in order to

    A. permit reducing the number of runs on the track
    B. alert the motormen operating on the track that maintainers are at work
    C. permit notifying passengers of possible delays
    D. facilitate delivery of materials required by the maintainers

17. The following are duties of the quality control section in the car maintenance department. The following possible duties are offered for your consideration.
    I. Sets procedures for the inspection and repair of car equipment
    II. Insures accepted level of performance in car repairs
    III. Analyzes and adjusts signal system failures
    IV. Investigates and approves new car equipment
    V. Conducts research and development on car equipment
    VI. Insures maintenance of production quotas in car repairs
    VII. Monitors savings due to reduction in overtime

    Which of the following suggested answers describes the duties of the quality control section?

    A. I, II, III
    B. I, II, III, IV
    C. I, II, IV, V
    D. I, II, III, VI, VII

18. When the thermal switch on an R-44 door operator motor is open, the door will

    A. remain closed at all times
    B. remain open at all times
    C. operate at a speed slower than normal
    D. operate at a speed faster than normal

19. For you to fulfill the duties and responsibilities which are inherent in your position and in order to gain the full approval of your superior, there are certain basic essentials that you must master.
    The following are offered for your consideration as being possible essentials which you should master in order to relate effectively to your superior.
    Understanding
    I. your duties and assuming your responsibilities
    II. the needs of your superior for information feedback from you
    III. the preferences of your superior
    IV. the desire of your superior to be friendly with you
    Of the following suggested answers, the one which describes the ESSENTIALS that should be mastered is

    A. I only   B. II only
    C. I, IV   D. I, II, III

20. Diesel-engine operated locomotives in the transit system are used PRIMARILY for the

    A. inspection of track conditions
    B. removal of snow
    C. moving of trains in and out of the inspection barns
    D. work trains in the maintenance of way department

21. The coupler electric portion contact carrier provides a means whereby the control cable of one car may be readily connected to that of another car.
    The following devices are offered for your consideration as being possibly controlled through the coupler electric portion contact carrier.
    I. Traction motor
    II. Door control
    III. Electro-pneumatic brake control
    IV. Fan and heater control
    V. Interior light control
    Of the following suggested answers, the one that identifies the devices controlled through the electric coupler portion is

    A. I, II   B. II, III
    C. II, III, IV   D. I, II, III, IV, V

22. The M-3-A lead valve used on the SMEE equipment is preset to automatically maintain a pressure of _____ psi.

    A. 85   B. 95   C. 110   D. 125

23. The ME-23 brake valve is used on cars provided with the

    A. UE-5 brake equipment   B. M-3-A feed valve
    C. A-1 operating unit   D. A-3 compressor unit

24. The derailment-collision committee consists of designated members of the following departments: maintenance of way (track and signal), car maintenance, transportation, engineering, and

   A. station   B. power   C. legal   D. safety

25. Subway cars are equipped with air compressors to operate the pneumatic equipment. The moisture in the compressed air is condensed in the compressor reservoir and is discharged

   A. by the road car inspector periodically by opening the drain valve
   B. by the motorman at the terminal before the start of the run
   C. automatically with each operating cycle of the compressor governor
   D. automatically as a vapor with the use of a high voltage heating coil

26. On the R-10 to R-40 type cars, the motors of the electric door operators are supplied with

   A. 32 volts DC   B. 115 volts AC
   C. 300 volts DC   D. 600 volts DC

Questions 27-28.

DIRECTIONS: Questions 27 and 28 are based on the following paragraph.

The car maintenance department is considering the purchase of a certain car part from Manufacturer X for $210. An equivalent part can be purchased from Manufacturer Y for $150. The part made by Manufacturer X must be reconditioned every 3 years using material that costs $45 and requires 6 hours of labor. The part made by Manufacturer Y must be reconditioned every 1 1/2 years using material that costs $36 and requires 5 hours of labor. The maintainer's rate of pay is $18 per hour.

27. The cost of operating with the part made by Manufacturer X (excluding the first cost) is MOST NEARLY _____ per year.

   A. $45   B. $48   C. $51   D. $63

28. The total cost of operating with the part made by Manufacturer Y over a period of 12 years, including the first cost of the part and assuming the part is scrapped at the end of 12 years, is MOST NEARLY

   A. $708   B. $858   C. $1,032   D. $1,158

29. You have been requested by your superior to investigate the cause of the poor finish and out of tolerance condition of the wheels machined on the wheel truing machine in the shop. You are told that this is an urgent job and that a written report is desired giving the correct actions to be taken to solve the problem.
The following characteristics of a written report which would be of greatest value to your superior are offered for your consideration.
   I. Detailed description of the problem
   II. Brief description of the problem
   III. Descriptions of possible solutions
   IV. Recommended corrective actions
   V. Detailed sketches of the wheels and of the wheel truing machine

Of the following suggested answers, the one that describes a report of GREATEST value to your superior is

A. I, III
B. II, IV
C. I, III, IV
D. I, III, IV, V

30. The Atlas Crane cars use General Motors 6-cylinder, V-type, 2-stroke cycle engines. One of these engines is operating with a low air box pressure resulting in inefficient combustion and scavenging.
The following faults are offered for your consideration as being possibly responsible for the low air box pressure.
    I. High air inlet restrictions
    II. Damaged blower rotors
    III. Clogged blower air inlet screen
    IV. High exhaust back pressure
Of the following suggested answers, the one that describes the CAUSES of the low air box pressure is

A. I, II
B. I, II, III
C. I, II, IV
D. II, III, IV

KEY (CORRECT ANSWERS)

1.	C	16.	B
2.	D	17.	C
3.	D	18.	C
4.	C	19.	D
5.	C	20.	D
6.	D	21.	D
7.	C	22.	C
8.	B	23.	A
9.	B	24.	D
10.	C	25.	C
11.	B	26.	A
12.	B	27.	C
13.	C	28.	C
14.	D	29.	B
15.	C	30.	B

SAFETY
EXAMINATION SECTION
TEST 1

DIRECTIONS: Each question or incomplete statement is followed by several suggested answers or completions. Select the one that BEST answers the question or completes the statement. *PRINT THE LETTER OF THE COREECT ANSWER IN THE SPACE AT THE RIGHT.*

1. When carrying pipe, employees are cautioned against lifting with the fingers inserted in the ends.
   The PROBABLE reason for this caution is to avoid the possibility of

   A. dropping and damaging pipe
   B. getting dirt and perspiration on the inside of the pipe
   C. cutting the fingers on the edge of the pipe
   D. straining finger muscles

   1.____

2. The MOST common cause for a workman to lose his balance and fall when working from an extension ladder is

   A. too much spring in the ladder
   B. sideways sliding of the top
   C. exerting a heavy pull on an object which gives suddenly
   D. working on something directly behind the ladder

   2.____

3. It is NOT necessary to wear protective goggles when

   A. drilling rivet holes in a steel beam
   B. sharpening tools on a power grinder
   C. welding a steel plate to a pipe column
   D. laying up a cinder block partition

   3.____

4. On your first day on the job as a helper, you are assigned to work with a maintainer. During the course of the work, you realize that the maintainer is about to violate a basic safety rule.
   In this case, the BEST thing for you to do is to

   A. immediately call it to his attention
   B. say nothing until he actually violates the rule and then call it to his attention
   C. say nothing, but later report this action to the foreman
   D. walk away from him so that you will not become involved

   4.____

5. Telephones are located alongside of the tracks for emergency use. The locations of these telephones are indicated by blue lights.
   The reason for selecting this color rather than green is that

   A. a blue light can be seen for greater distances
   B. blue lights are easier to buy
   C. green cannot be seen by a person who is color-blind
   D. green lights are used for train signals

   5.____

6. If it is necessary to lift up and hold one heavy part of a piece of equipment with a pinch bar so that there is enough clearance to work with the hands under the part, one IMPORTANT precaution is to

   A. wear gloves
   B. watch the bar to be ready if it slips
   C. work as fast as possible
   D. insert a temporary block to hold the part

7. The MOST important reason for insisting on neatness in maintenance quarters is that it

   A. increases the available storage space
   B. makes for good employee morale
   C. prevents tools from becoming rusty
   D. decreases the chances of accidents to employees

8. There are many steel ladders and stairways for the use of maintenance workers. Their GREATEST danger is that they

   A. have sharp edges causing cuts
   B. are slippery when greasy and wet
   C. cause colds
   D. have no *give* and thus cause fatigue

9. When using a brace and bit to bore a hole completely through a partition, it is MOST important to

   A. lean heavily on the brace and bit
   B. maintain a steady turning speed all through the job
   C. have the body in a position that will not be easily thrown off balance
   D. reverse the direction of the bit at frequent intervals

10. Flux is used when soldering two pieces of sheet metal together in order to

    A. conduct the heat of the soldering iron to the sheets
    B. lower the melting point of the solder
    C. glue the solder to the sheets
    D. protect the sheet metal from oxidizing when heated by the soldering iron

11. A rule of the transit system states that in walking on the track, walk opposite the direction of traffic on that track if possible.
    By logical reasoning, the PRINCIPAL safety idea behind this rule is that the man on the track

    A. is more likely to see an approaching train
    B. will be seen more readily by the motorman
    C. need not be as careful
    D. is better able to judge the speed of the train

12. An outstanding cause of accidents is the improper use of tools.
    The MOST helpful conclusion you can draw from this statement is that

    A. most tools are defective
    B. many accidents involving the use of tools occur because of poor working habits

C. most workers are poorly trained
D. many accidents involving the use of tools are unavoidable

13. An employee is required to make a written report of any unusual occurrence promptly. The BEST reason for requiring promptness is that

    A. it helps prevent similar occurrences
    B. the employee is less likely to forget details
    C. there is always a tendency to do a better job under pressure
    D. the report may be too long if made at an employee"s convenience

14. There are a few workers who are seemingly prone to accidents and who, regardless of their assigned job, have a higher accident rate than the average worker.
    If your co-worker is known to be such an individual, the BEST course for you to pursue would be to

    A. do most of the assigned work yourself
    B. refuse to work with this individual
    C. provide him with a copy of all rules and regulations
    D. personally check all safety precautions on each job

15. When summoning an ambulance for an injured person, it is MOST important to give the

    A. name of the injured person
    B. nature of the injuries
    C. cause of the accident
    D. location of the injured person

16. The MOST likely cause of accidents involving minor injuries is

    A. careless work practices
    B. lack of safety devices
    C. inferior equipment and materials
    D. insufficient safety posters

17. In an accident report, the information which may be MOST useful in decreasing the recurrence of similar-type accidents is the

    A. extent of injuries sustained
    B. time the accident happened
    C. number of people involved
    D. cause of the accident

18. Before a newly-riveted connection can be approved, the rivets should be struck with a light hammer in order to

    A. improve the shape of the rivet heads
    B. knock off any rust or burnt metal
    C. detect any loose rivets
    D. give the rivets a tighter fit

19. If the feet of a ladder are found to be resting on a slightly uneven surface, it would be BEST to

   A. move the ladder to an entirely different location
   B. even up the feet of the ladder with a small wedge
   C. get two men to bolster the ladder while it is being climbed
   D. get another ladder that is more suitable to the conditions

20. It would be POOR practice to hold a piece of wood in your hands or lap while you are tightening a screw in the wood because

   A. the wood would probably split
   B. sufficient leverage cannot be obtained
   C. the screwdriver may bend
   D. you might injure yourself

21. If a man on a job has to report an accident to the office by telephone, he should request the name of the person taking the call and also note the time.
The reason for this precaution is to fix responsibility for the

   A. entire handling of the accident thereafter
   B. accuracy of the report
   C. recording of the report
   D. preparation of the final written report

22. Employees of the transit system whose work requires them to enter upon the tracks are warned not to wear loose-fitting clothes.
The MOST important reason for this warning is that loose-fitting clothes may

   A. tear more easily than snug-fitting clothes
   B. give insufficient protection against dust
   C. catch on some projection of a passing train
   D. interfere when the men are using heavy tools

23. In case of accident, employees who witnessed the accident are required to make INDIVIDUAL written reports on prescribed forms as soon as possible.
The MOST logical reason for requiring such individual reports rather than a single, joint report signed by all witnesses is that the individual reports are

   A. *less* likely to be lost at the same time
   B. *more* likely to result in reducing the number of accidents
   C. *less* likely to contain unnecessary information
   D. *more* likely to give the complete picture

24. The logical reason that certain employees who work on the tracks carry small parts in fiber pails rather than in steel pails is that fiber pails

   A. can't be dented by rough usage
   B. do not conduct electricity
   C. are stronger
   D. can't rust

25. Maintenance workers whose duties require them to work on the tracks generally work in pairs.
The LEAST likely of the following possible reasons for this practice is that

    A. the men can help each other in case of accident
    B. it protects against vandalism
    C. some of the work requires two men
    D. there is usually too much equipment for one man to carry

25.____

KEY (CORRECT ANSWERS)

1.	C	11.	A
2.	C	12.	B
3.	D	13.	B
4.	A	14.	D
5.	D	15.	D
6.	D	16.	A
7.	D	17.	D
8.	B	18.	C
9.	C	19.	B
10.	D	20.	D

21. C
22. C
23. D
24. B
25. B

TEST 2

DIRECTIONS: Each question or incomplete statement is followed by several suggested answers or completions. Select the one that BEST answers the question or completes the statement. *PRINT THE LETTER OF THE CORRECT ANSWER IN THE SPACE AT THE RIGHT.*

1. Safety-mindedness cannot be achieved by command; it must be developed. Assume that you will be responsible for informing and training your subordinates in proper safety procedures.
   Which of the following methods is the MOST effective means of developing proper concern for safety among your subordinates?

   A. Award prizes for the best safety slogans
   B. Issue monthly safety bulletins
   C. Establish a safety suggestion program
   D. Hold periodic, informal group meetings on safety

   1.____

2. Of the following, the MAIN purpose of a safety training program for employees is to

   A. fix the blame for accidents
   B. describe accidents which have occurred
   C. hold the employees responsible for unsafe working conditions
   D. make the employees aware of the basic causes of accidents

   2.____

3. When administering first aid to a person suffering from shock as a result of an accident, of the following, it is MOST important to

   A. cover the person and keep him warm
   B. apply artificial respiration
   C. prop him up in a sitting position
   D. massage the person in order to aid blood circulation

   3.____

4. Assume you have just been appointed. You notice that certain equipment which is assigned to you is defective and that use of this equipment may eventually result in unnecessary costs and perhaps injury to you.
   The BEST thing for you to do is to

   A. speak to the maintenance men in the project about repairing the equipment
   B. discuss the matter with your foreman
   C. mind your own business since you have just been appointed
   D. speak to other workers and find out if they had any experience with defective equipment

   4.____

5. Assume you are working in a project building and one of the housing caretakers has just been seriously injured in an accident in the slop sink room.
   Your FIRST concern should be to

   A. help the injured man
   B. find the cause of the accident
   C. report the accident to your foreman
   D. report the accident to the caretaker's boss

   5.____

40

6. Assume a mass of extension cords plugged into one outlet in a shop results in overloading the electrical circuit and causes a fire.
   Which of the following types of extinguisher should be used to put out the fire?

   A. Carbon dioxide (CO_2)
   B. Water
   C. Soda acid
   D. Carbon tetrachloride

   6._____

7. Manufacturers of chemicals usually recommend that special precautions be taken when the chemicals are used.
   Of the following, which one would a manufacturer be LEAST likely to recommend?

   A. Wear leather gloves
   B. Wear a respirator
   C. Wear safety goggles
   D. Have a first aid kit available

   7._____

Questions 8-10.

DIRECTIONS: Questions 8 through 10 consist of groups of statements that have to do with safety precautions and procedures. Choose the statement in each group that is NOT correct.

8. A. The label on the original container of the pesticide should be read before each use.
    B. Pest control equipment should be cleaned regularly.
    C. Whenever there is a choice of chemicals, the chemical which is less hazardous to humans should be used at all times.
    D. For the transfer of concentrates from drums, either threaded taps or drum pumps should be used.

    8._____

9. A. Do not use a petroleum base on an asphalt tile floor.
    B. Do not spray oil base sprays on material colored with oil soluble dyes.
    C. Do not use respirators.
    D. Do not use pesticides which are highly poisonous to mammals.

    9._____

10. (The following statements deal with disposal of empty containers which hold highly toxic organic phosphate insecticides.)

    A. Do not reuse these containers.
    B. Pour one pint of water into the empty container, add bicarbonate of soda, and bury the container of rinse solution at least 18 inches below ground.
    C. Wet all inner surfaces with the proper rinse solution.
    D. Punch holes in the top and bottom of the can, crush the can, and bury deeply in an isolated location.

    10._____

11. A good first-aid treatment to administer to a man who has apparently been rendered unconscious by a high voltage shock would be to

    A. give him a stimulant by mouth
    B. apply artificial respiration if he is not breathing
    C. apply artificial respiration as a precautionary measure even if he is breathing
    D. keep him warm and comfortable

    11._____

12. A contributing cause present in practically all accidents is

    A. failure to give close attention to the job at hand
    B. lack of cooperation among the men in a gang
    C. failure to place the right man in the right job
    D. use of improper tools

13. Safety requires that wood ladders be unpainted.
    The PROBABLE reason for this is that paint

    A. is inflammable
    B. may deteriorate wood
    C. makes ladder rungs slippery
    D. may cover cracks or defects

14. If you notice one of your helpers doing a job in an unsafe manner and he tells you that this is the way the maintainer told him to do it, you should FIRST

    A. speak to this maintainer and find out if the helper was telling you the truth
    B. reprimand the helper for violating safety rules
    C. question this maintainer to see if he knows the safe way to do the job
    D. show the helper the correct method and see that he does the job properly

15. If a person has a deep puncture in his finger caused by a sharp nail, the BEST immediate first-aid procedure would be to

    A. encourage bleeding by exerting pressure around the injured area
    B. stop all bleeding
    C. prevent air from reaching the wound
    D. probe the wound for steel particles

16. It is MOST important to give complete details of an accident on the accident report because this will

    A. cause the injured employee to be more careful in the future
    B. keep supervision informed of the working conditions
    C. help in the defense against spurious compensation claims
    D. provide information to help avoid future accidents

17. A transit employee equipped with only a white flashlight, who wishes to stop a train because of an emergency, should face the train and wave the light in a

    A. vertical line
    B. vertical circle
    C. horizontal line
    D. forward and backward direction

18. The employee who opens a first-aid kit must make an immediate report on a prescribed form.
    Such report would NOT show the

    A. name of the employee opening the kit
    B. last previous date on which the kit was used

C. purpose for which the materials therein were used
D. amount of first aid material used

19. Carbon tetrachloride fire extinguishers have been replaced by dry chemical fire extinguishers MAINLY because the carbon tetrachloride is

    A. toxic
    B. not as effective
    C. frequently pilfered for cleaning purposes
    D. not readily available

20. The BEST first-aid for a man who has no external injury but is apparently suffering from internal injury due to an accident is to

    A. take him immediately to a doctor's office
    B. administer a stimulant
    C. cover him with a blanket and immediately summon a doctor or ambulance
    D. administer artificial respiration

21. While your men were working on the plumbing of a station toilet, a passenger tripped over some of your material on the platform.
    In making a report of the accident, the LEAST necessary item to include is the

    A. time of day
    B. distance from the entrance turnstile to the toilet
    C. date of occurrence
    D. condition of the platform when the accident occurred

22. All employees witnessing an accident are required to make a written report as soon as possible describing what they witnessed.
    The MOST likely reason for requiring these reports in writing and as soon as possible is to

    A. make sure no witnesses are overlooked
    B. be able to correct the reports without delay
    C. get as many facts as possible on record before they are forgotten
    D. relieve supervision of the time consuming job of verbally questioning all witnesses

23. Of the following, the type of fire extinguisher which should be used on electrical fires is the _____ type.

    A. foam
    B. soda-acid
    C. pumped-water
    D. dry chemical

24. The PRIMARY purpose of an emergency alarm is to

    A. test circuits to see if they are alive
    B. provide a means of removing power from the third rail
    C. inform the trainmaster that trains cannot run in his zone
    D. inform maintenance crews working on the tracks that an emergency exists

25. In regard to flagging signals, which of the following statements is TRUE? 25.____
    A. A red flag must never be used to give a proceed signal to a motorman.
    B. Under all conditions, only a red flag or lamp can be used as a signal to the motorman to stop the train.
    C. After stopping a train, if a flagman wishes to signal the motorman to resume his normal speed, he should wave a yellow flag.
    D. Under normal flagging conditions, moving a white light up and down slowly is a signal to the motorman to resume normal speed and that the motorman should be prepared to stop within his range of vision.

KEY (CORRECT ANSWERS)

1. D
2. D
3. A
4. B
5. A

6. A
7. A
8. C
9. C
10. B

11. B
12. A
13. D
14. D
15. A

16. D
17. C
18. B
19. A
20. C

21. B
22. C
23. D
24. B
25. A

EXAMINATION SECTION
TEST 1

DIRECTIONS: Each question or incomplete statement is followed by several suggested answers or completions. Select the one that BEST answers the question or completes the statement. *PRINT THE LETTER OF THE CORRECT ANSWER IN THE SPACE AT THE RIGHT.*

1. All of the following statements concerning artificial respiration are true EXCEPT: 1.____
    A. Generally, water victims recover normal respiration more rapidly than victims of electric shock
    B. Artificial respiration is almost always ineffective when it is carried on for more than five minutes
    C. The effects of shock on a victim of a water accident are likely to be insignificant, particularly if the day is warm
    D. Artificial respiration is not likely to be effective in cases of carbon monoxide poisonin

2. Assume that you cut your hand slightly while working in your office. Of the following, the BEST thing for you to do would be to 2.____
    A. clean the cut when you get home that evening
    B. fill out an accident report
    C. notify your supervisor
    D. wash the cut and put a bandaid on it

3. If a person has an object caught in his throat or air passage but is breathing adequately, which one of the following should you do? 3.____
    A. Probe for the object.
    B. Force him to drink water.
    C. Lay him over your arm and slap him between the shoulder blades.
    D. Allow him to cough and to assume the position he finds most comfortable.

4. All of the following statements concerning simple fainting are true EXCEPT: 4.____
    A. Fainting can be prevented by having the patient lie flat with the head low
    B. Applying a whiff of ammonia is the most important step in first aid treatment
    C. Fainting is believed to be a reaction of the nervous system
    D. To get into position for swimming from the feet-first-dive, bend forward at the waist and pull the knees up

5. Of the following, the reason why infected wounds should be treated by immobilizing the part is PRIMARILY to 5.____
    A. protect from further injury through contact with objects
    B. lessen soreness or pain
    C. promote healing
    D. retard the spread of infection

45

6. Of the following, according to the American Red Cross, the preferred method of artificial respiration is the

   A. chest pressure-arm lift (Silvester) method
   B. back pressure-arm lift (Holgen-Nielsen) method
   C. Schaefer prone method
   D. mouth-to-mouth method

7. Of the following, the BEST first aid treatment for a cleaner who has burned his hand with dry caustic lye crystals is to

   A. wash his hand with large quantities of warm water
   B. brush his hand lightly with a soft, clean brush and wrap it in a clean rag
   C. place his hand in a mild solution of ammonia and cool water
   D. wash his hand with large quantities of cold water

8. If a co-worker is not breathing after receiving an electric shock but is no longer in contact with the electricity, it is MOST important for you to

   A. avoid moving him
   B. wrap the victim in a blanket
   C. force him to take hot liquids
   D. start artificial respiration promptly

9. The BEST IMMEDIATE first aid if a chemical solution splashes into the eyes is to

   A. protect the eyes from the light by bandaging
   B. flush the eyes with large quantities of clean water
   C. cause tears to flow by staring at a bright light
   D. rub the eyes dry with a towel

10. The BEST immediate first aid treatment for a scraped knee is to

    A. apply plain vaseline
    B. use a knee splint
    C. apply heat
    D. wash it with soap and water

11. Artificial respiration after a severe electric shock is ALWAYS necessary when the shock results in

    A. unconsciousness B. stoppage of breathing
    C. bleeding   D. a burn

12. If a person has a deep puncture in his finger caused by a sharp nail, the BEST immediate first aid procedure would be to

    A. prevent air from reaching the wound
    B. stop all bleeding
    C. encourage bleeding by exerting pressure around the injured area
    D. probe the wound for steel particles

13. When giving first aid to an injured person, which one of the following should you NOT do?

    A. Administer medication internally
    B. Send for a physician
    C. Control bleeding
    D. Treat for shock

14. Of the following, the BEST action to take to help someone whose eyes have been splashed with lye is to FIRST

    A. wash out the eyes with clean water
    B. wash out the eyes with a salt water solution
    C. apply a sterile dressing over the eyes
    D. do nothing to the eyes, but telephone for medical help

15. One of your men on the job is injured at a work site and is unconscious. The BEST course of action for you to follow is to

    A. give him liquids to drink
    B. have him remain in a lying position until medical help arrives
    C. immediately move him to the first aid station
    D. attempt to arouse him to consciousness by shaking him

16. A stock assistant accidentally spatters acid into his eye. First aid treatment for the eye should consist of the immediate application of

    A. cold water   B. a bandage
    C. baking soda   D. vaseline

17. The one of the following that is the PROPER first aid to administer to a conscious person suffering from chlorine inhalation is

    A. an alcoholic drink B. black coffee
    C. a pulmotor   D. a cold shower

18. Artificial respiration is the FIRST action you should take when a man becomes unconscious either as a result of drowning or as a result of

    A. chlorine poisoning B. electric shock
    C. falling   D. clothing catching fire

19. Assume that one of your co-workers has suffered an electric shock. Artificial respiration should be started on him immediately if he is

    A. unconscious and breathing
    B. conscious and in a daze
    C. unconscious and not breathing
    D. conscious and badly burned

20. Assume that one of your assistants was near the Freon 11 refrigeration system when a liquid Freon line ruptured. Some of the liquid Freon 11 has gotten into your assistant's right eye. Of the following actions, the one which you should NOT take is to

    A. immediately call for an eye specialist (medical doctor)
    B. gently and quickly rub the Freon 11 out of the eye

C. use a boric acid solution to clean out the Freon 11 from his eye
D. wash the eye by gently blowing the Freon 11 out of his eye with air

21. If an assistant stockman receives a burn but his skin does not blister, you should FIRST

    A. apply cold water to the burn
    B. write out the accident report
    C. send the man home to rest
    D. assign the man to a less strenuous job for the rest of the day

22. When mouth-to-mouth resuscitation is administered to an adult, the RECOMMENDED breathing rate of the rescuer is

    A. 4 breaths per minute
    B. 12 breaths per minute
    C. 25 breaths per minute
    D. 35 breaths per minute

23. In the winter while working in the field in a park area, a drowning man is pulled out of a lake. He is not breathing when rescued. The FIRST thing to do to the victim is to

    A. remove his wet clothes and put him in a blanket
    B. bring him to a warm shelter
    C. remove water from his lungs
    D. give him mouth-to-mouth resuscitation

24. The BEST way to treat a person who has fainted is to

    A. place him gently on his back
    B. give him a cold glass of water to drink
    C. give him artificial respiration
    D. revive him immediately by placing him in a sitting position

25. The BEST thing to do immediately for a person who has suffered a severe blow to his head in a fall is to

    A. have him lie down and remain quiet until medical attention is obtained
    B. quickly transport him to a bed
    C. have him sit down and give him a glass of water
    D. get him up and walk him around

KEY (CORRECT ANSWERS)

1. A
2. D
3. D
4. B
5. D

6. D
7. D
8. D
9. B
10. D

11. B
12. C
13. A
14. A
15. B

16. A
17. B
18. B
19. C
20. B

21. A
22. B
23. D
24. A
25. A

TEST 2

DIRECTIONS: Each question or incomplete statement is followed by several suggested answers or completions. Select the one that BEST answers the question or completes the statement. *PRINT THE LETTER OF THE CORRECT ANSWER IN THE SPACE AT THE RIGHT.*

1. In the case of severe bleeding from a hand, the first aider should IMMEDIATELY

    A. locate the pressure point above the wound and apply digital pressure at that point
    B. apply pressure directly on the wound with clean gauze or a towel
    C. apply a tourniquet in order to limit the flow of blood from the artery to the wound
    D. locate the pressure point and apply a tourniquet at that point

1.____

2. The UNIVERSAL antidote to be administered in poisoning cases if no specific antidote is known consists of

    A. several teaspoonfuls of baking soda in half a glass of water
    B. a large glass of milk diluted with an equal amount of water
    C. one part tea, two parts crumbled burnt toast, one part milk of magnesia
    D. one part milk, one part egg white, one part water

2.____

3. Of the following concerning mouth-to-mouth resuscitation, the operator can BEST be sure that no obstruction exists in the victim's air passage by following his first blowing efforts with a

    A. sharp tilt backward of the victim's head so that the chin points almost directly upward
    B. forceful opening of the victim's mouth as the victim's nostrils are held in a closed position
    C. removal of his mouth by turning his head to the side in order to listen for the return rush of air from the victim's body
    D. removal of mucous and foreign matter in the victim's mouth

3.____

4. If a particle is on the eyeball, one should NOT

    A. close his eyes for a few minutes in order to allow the tears to wash out the foreign matter
    B. grasp the lashes of the upper lid and draw it out and down over the lower lid in order to dislodge the particle
    C. use an eye dropper in order to flush the eye so that the particle will float out of the eye
    D. examine the eye in order to determine the location of the foreign particle and, when found, remove it from the eyeball by touching lightly with the moistened corner of a clean handkerchief

4.____

5. An examination of the victim's eyes following an injury discloses that the pupils are unequal in size. Of the following, this is MOST apt to indicate

    A. an injury to the retina
    B. a fractured skull
    C. a concussion
    D. an injury to the pupils

5.____

6. In dealing with an external wound, the first and most important thing to do is to stop severe bleeding. Of the following, the CHIEF justification for this statement is that

   A. death can result from too much loss of blood
   B. external wounds are sometimes more serious than internal wounds
   C. infection will set in if bleeding is not stopped
   D. severe bleeding is evidence that an artery has been cut

7. In the event of an emergency need for an ambulance, we should FIRST call the

   A. police
   B. hospital
   C. board of health
   D. fire department

8. In the case of a sprained ankle, an INCORRECT procedure in first aid would be to

   A. elevate the sprained part
   B. apply cold applications
   C. massage the part to restore circulation
   D. apply a temporary support

9. Of the following, the one which is NOT a symptom of shock is

   A. cool, clammy skin
   B. weak pulse
   C. flushed face
   D. feeling of weakness

10. The BEST emergency measure in a case where poison has been swallowed is to

    A. give an antiseptic
    B. give an emetic
    C. put hot applications on the stomach
    D. administer a stimulant

11. Digital pressure is used

    A. to restore consciousness in cases of white unconsciousness
    B. to control arterial bleeding
    C. after a tourniquet has been applied and has failed its purpose
    D. on the wound itself in case of a compound fracture

12. The INCORRECT procedure in treating nosebleed is to

    A. have the victim lie down immediately
    B. press the nostrils firmly together
    C. apply a large, cold, wet cloth to the nose
    D. pack the nose gently with gauze

13. A person who has fainted should be

    A. propped up on a pillow or head rest
    B. laid flat and kept quiet
    C. given a warm drink
    D. aroused as soon as possible

14. If, during a playground activity, a person loses consciousness, he is NOT suffering from heat exhaustion if his

    A. face is pale
    B. pulse is weak and rapid
    C. skin is cold and clammy
    D. face is flushed

15. A person during an epileptic seizure should be

    A. held securely so that he will not struggle
    B. left where he has fallen
    C. carried to the rest room
    D. given a stimulant

16. A sharp-edged instrument would MOST likely cause a(n) _____ wound.

    A. abrased   B. punctured   C. lacerated   D. incised

17. The MAIN objective in first aid care for a victim of poison by mouth is to

    A. first induce vomiting
    B. dilute the poison
    C. give an antidote
    D. look around for tell-tale evidence of the poison

18. With victims of shock, when medical help is not immediate, water should NOT be given to those who have

    A. suffered marked bleeding
    B. burns involving more than ten percent of the body surface
    C. a penetrating abdominal wound
    D. a fracture of the femur

19. The INCORRECT association of first aid bandage and body area of use is:

    A. Four-tailed bandage - nose
    B. Cravat bandage - knee
    C. Triangular bandage - head
    D. Figure-eight bandage - chest

20. A passenger has fallen on the platform and apparently broken a leg. Before calling for an ambulance, it would be BEST to

    A. make him comfortable where he has fallen
    B. apply a tourniquet
    C. move him to a nearby bench and make him comfortable
    D. ask him about the details of the accident

21. The recommended first aid procedure for a person who has fainted is to lay him down with his head lower than his body. Such a position is used because it

    A. quickly relieves exhaustion
    B. is the most comfortable position

C. speeds the return of blood to his head
D. retards rapid breathing

22. In first aid, splints would be used for

    A. an infection
    B. a bruise
    C. an open cut
    D. a broken bone

23. In treating a cut finger, the FIRST action should be to

    A. apply antiseptic
    B. wash it
    C. bandage it
    D. apply a splint

24. The method of artificial respiration that is considered to be the MOST satisfactory today is the

    A. mouth to mouth
    B. back-pressure arm-lift
    C. prone-pressure
    D. barrel roll

25. A cut finger should be washed with soap and water MAINLY because this

    A. reduces the possibility of infection
    B. increases the flow of blood
    C. stops the flow of blood
    D. stops abrasion

KEY (CORRECT ANSWERS)

1.	B	11.	B
2.	C	12.	A
3.	C	13.	B
4.	D	14.	D
5.	B	15.	B
6.	A	16.	D
7.	A	17.	B
8.	C	18.	C
9.	C	19.	D
10.	B	20.	A

21. C
22. D
23. B
24. A
25. A

EXAMINATION SECTION
TEST 1

DIRECTIONS: Each question or incomplete statement is followed by several suggested answers or completions. Select the one that BEST answers the question or completes the statement. *PRINT THE LETTER OF THE CORRECT ANSWER IN THE SPACE AT THE RIGHT.*

1. A supervisor was given a booklet that showed a new work method that could save time. He didn't tell his men because he thought that they would get the booklet anyway.
   For the supervisor to have acted like this is a
   A. *good* idea, because he saves time and both of talking to the men
   B. *bad* idea, because he should make sure his men know about better work methods
   C. *good* idea, because the men would rather read about it themselves
   D. *bad* idea, because a supervisor should always show his men every memo he gets from higher authority

   1.____

2. A supervisor found it necessary to discipline two subordinates. One man had been operating his equipment in a wrong way, while the other man came to work late for three days in a row. The supervisor decided to talk to both men together.
   For the supervisor to deal with the problems in this way is a
   A. *good* idea because each man will learn about the difficulties of the other person and how to solve such difficulties
   B. *bad* idea because the supervisor should wait until he can bring a larger group together and save time in discussing such questions
   C. *good* idea because he will be able to get the men to see that their problems are related
   D. *bad* idea because he should meet with each man separately and give him his full attention

   2.____

3. A supervisor should try to make his men feel their jobs are important in order to
   A. get the men to say good things about their supervisor to his own superior
   B. get the men to think in terms of advancing to better jobs
   C. let higher management in the agency know that the supervisor is efficient
   D. help the men to be able to work more efficiently and enthusiastically

   3.____

4. A supervisor should know approximately how long it takes to do a particular kind of job CHIEFLY because he
   A. will know how much time to take if he has to do it himself
   B. will be able to tell his men to do it even faster
   C. can judge the performance of the person doing the job
   D. can retrain experienced employees in better work habits

   4.____

5. Supervisors often get their employees' opinions about better work methods because
   A. the men will know that they are respected
   B. the men would otherwise lose all their confidence in the supervisor
   C. the supervisor might find in this way a good suggestion he could use
   D. this is the best method for improvement of work methods

6. Right after you have trained your subordinates in doing a new job, you find that they seem to be doing all right, but that it will take them several days to finish. You also have several groups of men working at other locations.
   The MOST efficient way for you to make sure that the men continue doing the new job properly is to
   A. stay on that job with the men until it is finished just in case trouble develops
   B. visit the men every half hour until the job is done
   C. stay away from their job that day and visit the men the next day to ask them if they had any problems
   D. visit the men a few times each day until they finish the new job

7. Assume that one of your new employees is older than you are. You also think that he may be hard to get along with because he is older than you.
   The BEST way for you to avoid any problems with the older worker is for you to
   A. lay down the law immediately and tell the man he better not cause you any trouble
   B. treat the man just the way you would any other worker
   C. always ask the older worker for advice in the presence of all the men
   D. ignore the man entirely until he realizes that you are the boss

8. Assume that you have tried a new method suggested by one of your employees and find that it is easier and cheaper than the method you had been using.
   The PROPER thing for you to do NEXT is to
   A. say nothing to anyone but train your men to use the new method
   B. train your men to use the new method and tell your crew that you got the idea from one of the men
   C. continue using the old method because a supervisor should not use suggestions of his men
   D. have your crew learn the new method and take credit for the idea since you are the boss

9. Suppose you are a supervisor and your superior tells you that the way your men are doing a certain procedure is wrong and that you should re-train our men as soon as possible.
   When you begin to re-train the men, the FIRST thing you should do is to
   A. tell your men that a wrong procedure had been used and that a new method must be learned as a result
   B. train your employees in the new method with no explanation since you are the boss

C. tell the crew that your superior has just decided that everyone should learn a new method
D. tell the crew that your superior says your method is wrong but that you don't agree with this

10. It is BAD practice to criticize a man in front of the other men because
    A. people will think you are too strict
    B. it is annoying to anyone who walks by
    C. it is embarrassing to the man concerned
    D. it will antagonize the other men

11. A supervisor decides not to put his two best men on a work detail because he knows that they won't like it.
    For the supervisor to make the work assignment this way is a
    A. *good* idea because it is only fair to give your best men a break once in a while
    B. *bad* idea because you should treat all of your me fairly and not show favoritism
    C. *good* idea because you save the strength of these men for another job
    D. *bad* idea because more of the men should be exempted from the assignment

12. Suppose you are a supervisor and you find it inconvenient to obey an established procedure set by your agency. You think another procedure would be better.
    The BEST thing to do first about this procedure that you don't like is for you to
    A. obey the procedure even if you don't to and suggest your idea to your own supervisor
    B. disregard the procedure because a supervisor is supposed to have some privileges
    C. follow the procedure some of the time but ignore it when the men are not watching
    D. organize a group of other supervisors to get the procedure changed

13. A supervisor estimated that it would take his crew one workday per week to do a certain job each week. However, after a month he noticed that the job averaged two and a half days a week and this delayed other jobs that had to be done.
    The FIRST thing that the supervisor should do in this case is to
    A. call him men together and warn them that they will get a poor work evaluation if they do not work harder
    B. talk to each man personally, asking him to work harder on the job
    C. go back and study the maintenance job by himself to see if more men should be assigned to the job
    D. write his boss a report describing in detail how much time it is taking the men to do the job

14. An employee complains to you that some of the work assignments are too difficult to do alone.
Which of the following is the BEST way for you to handle this complaint?
   A. Go with him to see exactly what he does and why he finds it so difficult
   B. Politely tell the man that he has to do the job or be brought up on charges
   C. Tell the man to send his complaint to the head of your agency
   D. Sympathize with the man and give him easier jobs

15. The BEST way for a supervisor to keep control of his work assignments is to
   A. ask the men to report to him immediately when their jobs are finished
   B. walk around the buildings once a week and get a first-hand view of what is being done
   C. keep his ears open for problems and complaints, but leave the men aloe to do the work
   D. write up a work schedule and check it periodically against the actual work done

16. A supervisor made a work schedule for his men. At the bottom of it, he wrote, *No changes or exceptions will be made in this schedule for any reason.*
For the supervisor to have made this statement is
   A. *good*, because the men will respect the supervisor for his attitude
   B. *bad*, because there are emergencies and special situations that occur
   C. *good*, because each man will know exactly what is expected of him
   D. *bad*, because the men should expect that no changes will ever be made in the work schedule without written permission

17. Which one of the following would NOT be a result of a well-planned work schedule?
The schedule
   A. makes efficient use of the time of the staff
   B. acts as a checklist for an important job that might be left out
   C. will give an idea of the work to a substitute supervisor
   D. shows at a glance who the best men are

18. A new piece of equipment you have ordered is delivered. You are familiar with it, but the men under you who will use it do not know the equipment.
Of the following methods, which is the BEST to take in explaining to them how to operate this equipment?
   A. Ask the men to watch other crews using the equipment
   B. Show one reliable man how to operate the equipment and ask him to teach the other men
   C. Ask the men to read the instructions in the manual for the equipment
   D. Call the men together and show them how to operate the equipment

19. One supervisor assigns work to his men by calling his crew together each week and describing what has to be done that week. He then tells them to arrange individual assignments among themselves and to work as a team during the week.

This method of scheduling work is a
- A. *good* idea because this guarantees that the men will work together
- B. *bad* idea because responsibility for doing the job is poorly fixed
- C. *good* idea because the men will finish the job in less time, working together
- D. *bad* idea because the supervisor should always stay with his men

20. Suppose that an employee came to his supervisor with a problem concerning his assignment.
For the supervisor to listen to his problem is a
- A. *good* idea because a supervisor should always take time off to talk when one of his men wants to talk
- B. *bad* idea because the supervisor should not be bothered during the work day
- C. *good* idea because it is the job of the supervisor to deal with problems of job assignment
- D. *bad* idea because the employee could start annoying the supervisor with all sorts of problems

20.____

21. Suppose that on the previous afternoon you were looking for an experienced employee in order to give him an emergency job and he was missing from his job location. The next morning, he tells you that he got sick suddenly and had to go home, but could not tell you since you were not around. He has never done this before.
What should you do?
- A. Tell the man he is excused and that in such circumstances he did the wisest thing
- B. Bring the man up on charges because whatever he says he could still have notified you
- C. Have the man examined by a doctor to see if he really was sick the day before
- D. Explain to the mean that he should make every effort to tell you or to get a message to you if he must leave

21.____

22. An employee had a grievance and went to his supervisor about it. The employee was not satisfied with the way the supervisor tried to help him and told him so. Yet, the supervisor had done everything he could under the circumstances.
The PROPER action for the supervisor to take at this time is to
- A. politely tell the employee that there is nothing more for the supervisor to do about the problem
- B. let the employee know how he can bring his complaint to a higher authority
- C. tell the employee that he must solve the problem on his own since he did not want to follow the supervisor's advice
- D. suggest to the employee that he ask for another supervisor for assistance

22.____

23. In which of the following situations is it BEST to give your men spoken rather than written orders?
    A. You want your men to have a record of the instructions.
    B. Spoken instructions are less likely to be forgotten.
    C. An emergency situation has arisen in which there is no time to write up instructions.
    D. There are instructions on time and leave regulations which are complicated.

24. One of your employees tells you that a week ago he had a small accident on the job but he did not bother telling you because he was able to continue working.
    For the employee not to have told his supervisor about the accident was
    A. *good*, because the accident was a small one
    B. *bad*, because all accidents should be reported, no matter how small
    C. *good*, because the supervisor should be bothered only for important matters
    D. *bad*, because having an accident is one way to get excused for the day

25. For a supervisor to deal with each of his subordinate in exactly the same manner is
    A. *poor*, because each man presents a different problem and there is no one way of handling all problems
    B. *good*, because once a problem is handled with one man, he can handle another man with the same problem
    C. *poor*, because the men will resent it if they are not handled each in a better way than others
    D. *good*, because this assures fair and impartial treatment of each subordinate

KEY (CORRECT ANSWERS)

1.	B		11.	B
2.	D		12.	A
3.	D		13.	C
4.	C		14.	A
5.	C		15.	D
6.	D		16.	B
7.	B		17.	D
8.	B		18.	D
9.	A		19.	B
10.	C		20.	C

21.	D
22.	B
23.	C
24.	B
25.	A

TEST 2

DIRECTIONS: Each question or incomplete statement is followed by several suggested answers or completions. Select the one that BEST answers the question or completes the statement. *PRINT THE LETTER OF THE CORRECT ANSWER IN THE SPACE AT THE RIGHT.*

1. Jim Johnson has been on your staff for over four years. He has always been a conscientious and productive worker. About a month ago, his wife died; and since that time, his work performance has been very poor.
   As his supervisor, which one of the following is the BEST way for you to deal with this situation?
   A. Allow Jim as much time as he needs to overcome his grief and hope that his work performance improves
   B. Meet with Jim to discuss ways to improve his performance
   C. Tell Jim directly that you are more concerned with his work performance than with his personal problem
   D. Prepare disciplinary action on Jim as soon as possible

   1.____

2. You are responsible for the overall operation of a storehouse which is divided into two sections. Each section has its own supervisor. You have decided to make several complex changes in the storekeeping procedures which will affect both sections.
   Of the following, the BEST way to make sure that these changes are understood by the two supervisors is for you to
   A. meet with both supervisors to discuss the changes
   B. issue a memorandum to each supervisor explaining the changes
   C. post the changes where the supervisors are sure to see them
   D. instruct one supervisor to explain the changes to the other supervisor

   2.____

3. You have called a meeting of all your subordinates to tell them what has to be done on a new project in which they will all be involved. Several times during the meeting, you ask if there are any questions about what you have told them.
   Of the following, to ask the subordinates whether there are any questions during the meeting can BEST be described as
   A. *inadvisable*, because it interferes with their learning about the new project
   B. *advisable*, because you will find out what they don't understand and have a chance to clear up any problems they may have
   C. *inadvisable*, because it makes the meeting too long and causes the subordinates to lose interest in the new project
   D. *advisable*, because it gives you a chance to learn which of your subordinates are paying attention to what you say

   3.____

4. As a supervisor, you are responsible for seeing to it that absenteeism does not become a problem among your subordinates.
   Which one of the following is NOT an acceptable way of controlling the problem of excessive absences?

   4.____

A. Distribute a written statement to your staff on the policies regarding absenteeism in your organization
B. Arrange for workers who have the fewest absences to talk to those workers who have the most absences
C. Let your subordinates know that a record is being kept of all absences
D. Arrange for counseling of those employees who are frequently absent

5. One of your supervisors has been an excellent worker for the past two years. There are no promotion opportunities for this worker in the foreseeable future. Due to the city's present budget crisis, a salary increase is not possible.
Under the circumstances, which one of the following actions on your part would be MOST likely to continue to motivate this worker?
    A. Tell the worker that times are bad all over and jobs are hard to find
    B. Give the worker less work and easier assignments
    C. Tell the worker to try to look for a better paying job elsewhere
    D. Seek the worker's advice often and show that the suggestions provided are appreciated

6. As a supervisor in a warehouse, it is important that you use your available work force to its fullest potential.
Which one of the following actions on your part is MOST likely to increase the effectiveness of your work force?
    A. Assigning more workers to a job than the number actually needed
    B. Eliminating all job training to allow more time for work output
    C. Using your best workers on jobs that average workers can do
    D. Making sure that all materials and equipment used are maintained in good working order

7. You learn that your storage area will soon be undergoing changes which will affect the work of your subordinates. You decide not to tell your subordinates about what is to happen.
Of the following, your action can BEST be described as
    A. *wise*, because your subordinates will learn of the changes for themselves
    B. *unwise*, because your subordinates should be advised about what is to happen
    C. *wise*, because it is better for your subordinates to continue working without being disturbed by such news
    D. *unwise*, because the work of your subordinates will gradually slow down

8. In making plans for the operation of your unit, you are MOST likely to see these plans carried out successfully if you
    A. allow your staff to participate in developing these plans
    B. do not spend any time on the minor details of these plans
    C. base these plans on the past experiences of others
    D. allow these plans to interact with outside activities in other units

9. As a supervisor in charge of the total operation of a food supply warehouse, you find vandalism to be a potentially serious problem. On occasion, trespassers have gained entrance into the facility by climbing over an unprotected 8-foot fence surrounding the warehouse whose dimensions measure 100 feet by 100 feet.
Assuming that all of the following would be equally effective ways in preventing these breaches in security in the situation described above, which one would be LEAST costly?
   A. Using two trained guard dogs to roam freely throughout the facility at night
   B. Hiring a security guard to patrol the facility after working hours
   C. Installing tape razor wire on top of the fence surrounding the facility
   D. Installing an electronic burglar alarm system requiring the installation of a new fence

10. The area for which you have program responsibility has undergone recent changes. Your staff is now required to perform many new tasks, and morale is low.
The LEAST effective way for you to improve long-term staff morale would be to
   A. develop support groups to discuss problems
   B. involve staff in job development
   C. maintain a comfortable social environment within the group
   D. adequately plan and give assignments in a timely manner

11. As a supervisor in a large office, one of your subordinate supervisors stops you in the middle of the office and complains loudly that he is being treated unfairly. The rest of the staff ceases work and listens to the complaint.
The MOST appropriate action for you to take in this situation is to
   A. ignore this unprofessional behavior and continue on your way
   B. tell the supervisor that his behavior is unprofessional and he should learn how to conduct himself
   C. explain to the supervisor why you believe he is not being treated unfairly
   D. ask the supervisor to come to your office at a specific time to discuss the matter

12. You are told that one of your subordinates is distributing literature which attempts to recruit individuals to join a particular organization. Several workers complain that their rights are being violated.
Of the following, the BEST action for you to take FIRST is to
   A. ignore the situation because no harm is being done
   B. discuss the matter further with your supervisor
   C. ask the worker to stop distributing the literature
   D. tell the workers that they do not have to read the material

13. You have been assigned to develop a short training course for a recently issued procedure.
In designing this course, which of the following statements is the LEAST important for you to consider?

A. The learning experience must be interesting and meaningful in terms of the staff member's job.
B. The method of teaching must be strictly followed in order to develop successful learning experiences.
C. The course content should incorporate the rules and regulations of the agency.
D. The procedure should be consistent with the agency's objectives.

14. As a supervisor, there are several newly-promoted employees under your supervision. Each of these employees is subject to a probationary period PRIMARILY to
    A. assess the employee's performance to see if the employee should be retained or removed from the position
    B. give the employee the option to return to his former employment if the employee is unhappy in the new position
    C. give the employee an opportunity to learn the duties and responsibilities of the position
    D. judge the employee's potential for upward mobility in the future

14.____

15. An employee under your supervision rushes into your office to tell you he has just received a telephone bomb threat.
    As the administrative supervisor, the FIRST thing you should do is
    A. evacuate staff from the floor
    B. call the police and building security
    C. advise your administrator
    D. do a preliminary search

15.____

16. After reviewing the Absence Control form for a unit under your supervision, you find that one of your staff members has a fifth undocumented sick leave within a six-month period.
    In this situation, the FIRST action you should take is to
    A. discuss the seriousness of the matter with the staff member when he returns to work and fully document the details of the discussion
    B. review the case with the location director and warn the staff member that future use of sick leave will be punished
    C. submit the proper disciplinary forms to ensure that the staff member is penalized for excessive absences
    D. request that the timekeeper put the staff member on doctor's note restriction

16.____

17. A subordinate supervisor recently assigned to your office begins his first conference with you by saying that he has learned something that another supervisor is doing that you should know about.
    After hearing this statement, of the following, the BEST approach for you to take is to
    A. explain to the supervisor that the conference is to discuss his work and not that of his co-workers
    B. tell the supervisor that you do not encourage a spy system among the staff you supervise

17.____

C. tell the supervisor that you will listen to his report only if the other supervisor is present
D. allow the supervisor to continue talking until you have enough information to make a decision on how best to respond

18. Assume that you are a supervisor recently assigned to a new unit. You notice that, for the past few days, one of the employees in your unit whose work is about average has been stopping work at about four o'clock and has been spending the rest of the afternoon relaxing at his desk.
The BEST of the following actions for you to take in this situation is to
    A. assign more work to this employee since it is apparent that he does not have enough work to keep him busy
    B. observe the employee's conduct more closely for about ten days before taking any more positive action
    C. discuss the matter with the employee, pointing out to him how he can use the extra hour daily to raise the level of his job performance
    D. question the previous supervisor in charge of the unit in order to determine whether he had sanctioned such conduct when he supervised that unit

19. A new supervisor was assigned to your program four months ago. Although he tries hard, he has been unable to meet certain standards because he still has a lot to learn. As his supervisor, you are required to submit performance evaluations within a few days.
How would you rate this employee on the tasks where he fails to meet standards because of lack of experience?
    A. Satisfactory   B. Conditional
    C. Unsatisfactory   D. Unratable

20. You find that there is an important procedural error in a memo which you distributed to your staff several days ago.
The BEST approach for you to take at this time is to
    A. send a corrected memo to the staff, indicating what prior error was made
    B. send a corrected memo to the staff without mentioning the prior error
    C. tell the staff about the error at the next monthly staff meeting
    D. place the corrected memo on the office bulletin board

21. Your superior asks you, a supervisor, about the status of the response to a letter from a public official concerning a client's case. When you ask the subordinate who was assigned to prepare the response to give you the letter, the subordinate denies that it was given to him. You are certain that the subordinate has the letter, but is withholding it because the response has not yet been prepared.
Of the following, in order to secure the letter from the subordinate, you should FIRST
    A. accuse the subordinate of lying and demand that the letter be given to you immediately
    B. say that you would consider it a personal favor if the subordinate would find the letter

C. continue to question the subordinate until he admits to having been given the letter
D. offer a face-saving solution, such as asking the subordinate to look again for the letter

22. As a supervisor, you have been assigned to write a few paragraphs to be included in the agency's annual report, describing a public service agency department this year as compared to last year.
Which of the following elements basic to the agency is LEAST likely to have changed since last year?
    A. Mission   B. Structure   C. Technology   D. Personnel

23. As a supervisor, you have been informed that a grievance has been filed against you, accusing you of assigning a subordinate to out-of-title tasks.
Of the following, the BEST approach for you to take is to
    A. waive the grievance so that it will proceed to a Step II hearing
    B. immediately change the subordinate's assignment to avoid future problems
    C. respond to the grievance, giving appropriate reasons for the assignment
    D. review the job description to ensure that the subordinate's tasks are not out-of-title

24. Which of the following is NOT a correct statement about agency group training programs in a public service agency?
    A. Training sessions continue for an indefinite period of time.
    B. Group training sessions are planned for designated personnel.
    C. Training groups are organized formally through administrative planning.
    D. Group training is task-centered and aimed toward accomplishing specific educational goals.

25. As a supervisor, you have submitted a memo to your superior requesting a conference to discuss the performance of a manager under your supervision. The memo states that the manager has a good working relationship with her staff; however, she tends to interpret agency policy too liberally and shows poor administrative skills by missing some deadlines and not keeping proper controls.
Which of the following steps should NOT be taken in order to prepare for this conference with your superior?
    A. Collect and review all your notes regarding the manager's prior performance.
    B. Outline your agenda so that you will have sufficient time to discuss the situation.
    C. Tell the manager that you will be discussing her performance with your superior.
    D. Clearly define objectives which will focus on improving the manager's performance.

KEY (CORRECT ANSWERS)

1.	B	11.	D
2.	A	12.	C
3.	B	13.	B
4.	B	14.	A
5.	D	15.	B
6.	D	16.	A
7.	B	17.	D
8.	A	18.	C
9.	C	19.	B
10.	C	20.	A

21.	D
22.	A
23.	C
24.	A
25.	C

EXAMINATION SECTION
TEST 1

DIRECTIONS: Each question or incomplete statement is followed by several suggested answers or completions. Select the one that BEST answers the question or completes the statement. *PRINT THE LETTER OF THE CORRECT ANSWER IN THE SPACE AT THE RIGHT.*

1. Of the following, the one MOST important quality required of a good supervisor is
   A. ambition   B. leadership   C. friendliness   D. popularity

   1.____

2. It is often said that a supervisor can delegate authority but never responsibility. This means MOST NEARLY that
   A. a supervisor must do his own work if he expects it to be done properly
   B. a supervisor can assign someone else to do his work, but in the last analysis, the supervisor himself must take the blame for any actions followed
   C. authority and responsibility are two separate things that cannot be borne by the same person
   D. it is better for a supervisor never to delegate his authority

   2.____

3. One of your men who is a habitual complainer asks you to grant him a minor privilege.
   Before granting or denying such a request, you should consider
   A. the merits of the case
   B. that it is good for group morale to grant a request of this nature
   C. the man's seniority
   D. that to deny such a request will lower your standing with the men

   3.____

4. A supervisory practice on the part of a foreman which is MOST likely to lead to confusion and inefficiency is for him to
   A. give orders verbally directly to the man assigned to the job
   B. issue orders only in writing
   C. follow up his orders after issuing them
   D. relay his orders to the men through co-workers

   4.____

5. It would be POOR supervision on a foreman's part if he
   A. asked an experienced maintainer for his opinion on the method of doing a special job
   B. make it a policy to avoid criticizing a man in front of his co-workers
   C. consulted his assistant supervisor on unusual problems
   D. allowed a cooling-off period of several days before giving one of his men a deserved reprimand

   5.____

6. Of the following behavior characteristics of a supervisor, the one that is MOST likely to lower the morale of the men he supervises is
   A. diligence
   B. favoritism
   C. punctuality
   D. thoroughness

6._____

7. Of the following, the BEST method of getting an employee who is not working up to his capacity to produce more work is to
   A. have another employee criticize his production
   B. privately criticize his production but encourage him to produce more
   C. criticize his production before his associates
   D. criticize his production and threaten to fire him

7._____

8. Of the following, the BEST thing for a supervisor to do when a subordinate has done a very good job is to
   A. tell him to take it easy
   B. praise his work
   C. reduce his workload
   D. say nothing because he may become conceited

8._____

9. Your orders to your crew are MOST likely to be followed if you
   A. explain the reasons for these orders
   B. warn that all violators will be punished
   C. promise easy assignments to those who follow these orders best
   D. say that they are for the good of the department

9._____

10. In order to be a good supervisor, you should
    A. impress upon your men that you demand perfection in their work at all times
    B. avoid being blamed for your crew's mistakes
    C. impress your superior with your ability
    D. see to it that your men get what they are entitled to

10._____

11. In giving instructions to a crew, you should
    A. speak in as loud a tone as possible
    B. speak in a coaxing, persuasive manner
    C. speak quietly, clearly, and courteously
    D. always use the word *please* when giving instructions

11._____

12. Of the following factors, the one which is LEAST important in evaluating an employee and his work is his
    A. dependability
    B. quantity of work done
    C. quality of work done
    D. education and training

12._____

13. When a District Superintendent first assumes his command, it is LEAST important for him at the beginning to observe
    A. how his equipment is designed and its adaptability
    B. how to reorganize the district for greater efficiency
    C. the capabilities of the men in the district
    D. the methods of operation being employed

13._____

14. When making an inspection of one of the buildings under your supervision, the BEST procedure to follow in making a record of the inspection is to
    A. return immediately to the office and write a report from memory
    B. write down all the important facts during or as soon as you complete the inspection
    C. fix in your mind all important facts so that you can repeat them from memory if necessary
    D. fix in your mind all important facts so that you can make out your report at the end of the day

15. Assume that your superior has directed you to make certain changes in your established procedure. After using this modified procedure on several occasions, you find that the original procedure was distinctly superior and you wish to return to it.
    You should
    A. let your superior find this out for himself
    B. simply change back to the original procedure
    C. compile definite data and information to prove your case to your superior
    D. persuade one of the more experienced workers to take this matter up with your superior

16. An inspector visited a large building under construction. He inspected the soil lines at 9 A.M., water lines at 10 A.M., fixtures at 11 A.M., and did his office work in the afternoon. He followed the same pattern daily for weeks.
    This procedure was
    A. *good*, because it was methodical and he did not miss anything
    B. *good*, because it gave equal time to all phases of the plumbing
    C. *bad*, because not enough time was devoted to fixtures
    D. *bad*, because the tradesmen knew when the inspection would occur

17. Assume that one of the foremen in a training course, which you are conducting, proposes a poor solution for a maintenance problem.
    Of the following, the BEST course of action for you to take is to
    A. accept the solution tentatively and correct it during the next class meeting
    B. point out all the defects of this proposed solution and wait until somebody thinks of a better solution
    C. try to get the class to reject this proposed solution and develop a better solution
    D. let the matter pass since somebody will present a better solution as the class work proceeds

18. As a supervisor, you should be seeking ways to improve the efficiency of shop operations by means such as changing established work procedures.
    The following are offered as possible actions that you should consider in changing established work procedures:
    I. Make changes only when your foremen agree to them
    II. Discuss changes with your supervisor before putting them into practice

4 (#1)

III. Standardize any operation which is performed on a continuing basis
IV. Make changes quickly and quietly in order to avoid dissent
V. Secure expert guidance before instituting unfamiliar procedures
Of the following suggested answers, the one that describes the actions to be taken to change established work procedures is
   A. I, IV, V   B. II, III, V   C. III, IV, V   D. All of the above

19. A supervisor determined that a foreman, without informing his superior, delegated responsibility for checking time cards to a member of his gang. The supervisor then called the foreman into his office where he reprimanded the foreman.
This action of the supervisor in reprimanding the foreman was
   A. *proper*, because the checking of time cards is the foreman's responsibility and should not be delegated
   B. *proper*, because the foreman did not ask the supervisor for permission to delegate responsibility
   C. *improper*, because the foreman may no longer take the initiative in solving future problems
   D. *improper*, because the supervisor is interfering in a function which is not his responsibility

19.____

20. A capable supervisor should check all operations under his control.
Of the following, the LEAST important reason for doing this is to make sure that
   A. operations are being performed as scheduled
   B. he personally observes all operations at all times
   C. all the operations are still needed
   D. his manpower is being utilized efficiently

20.____

21. A supervisor makes it a practice to apply fair and firm discipline in all cases of rule infractions, including those of a minor nature.
This practice should PRIMARILY be considered
   A. *bad*, since applying discipline for minor violations is a waste of time
   B. *good*, because not applying discipline for minor infractions can lead to a more serious erosion of discipline
   C. *bad*, because employees do not like to be disciplined for minor violations of the rules
   D. *good*, because violating any rule can cause a dangerous situation to occur

21.____

22. A maintainer would PROPERLY consider it poor supervisory practice for a foreman to consult with him on
   A. which of several repair jobs should be scheduled first
   B. how to cope with personal problems at home
   C. whether the neatness of his headquarters can be improved
   D. how to express a suggestion which the maintainer plans to submit formally

22.____

5 (#1)

23. Assume that you have determined that the work of one of your foremen and the men he supervises is consistently behind schedule. When you discuss this situation with the foreman, he tells you that his men are poor workers and then complains that he must spend all of his time checking on their work.
The following actions are offered for your consideration as possible ways of solving the problem of poor performance of the foreman and his men:
I. Review the work standards with the foreman and determine whether they are realistic.
II. Tell the foreman that you will recommend him for the foreman's training course for retraining.
III. Ask the foreman for the names of the maintainers and then replace them as soon as possible.
IV. Tell the foreman that you expect him to meet a satisfactory level of performance.
V. Tell the foreman to insist that his men work overtime to catch up to the schedule.
VI. Tell the foreman to review the type and amount of training he has given the maintainers.
VII. Tell the foreman that he will be out of a job if he does not produce on schedule.
VIII. Avoid all criticism of the foreman and his methods.
Which of the following suggested answers CORRECTLY lists the proper actions to be taken to solve the problem of poor performance of the foreman and his men?
A. I, II, IV, VI   B. I, III, V, VII   C. II, III, VI, VIII   D. IV, V, VI, VIII

23.____

24. When a conference or a group discussion is tending to turn into a *bull session* without constructive purpose, the BEST action to take is to
A. reprimand the leader of the bull session
B. redirect the discussion to the business at hand
C. dismiss the meeting and reschedule it for another day
D. allow the bull session to continue

24.____

25. Assume that you have been assigned responsibility for a program in which a high production rate is mandatory. From past experience, you know that your foremen do not perform equally well in the various types of jobs given to them. Which of the following methods should you use in selecting foremen for the specific types of work involved in the program?
A. Leave the method of selecting foremen to your supervisor
B. Assign each foreman to the work he does best
C. Allow each foreman to choose his own job
D. Assign each foreman to a job which will permit him to improve his own abilities

25.____

KEY (CORRECT ANSWERS)

1.	B	11.	C
2.	B	12.	D
3.	A	13.	B
4.	D	14.	B
5.	D	15.	C
6.	B	16.	D
7.	B	17.	C
8.	B	18.	B
9.	A	19.	A
10.	D	20.	B

21.	B
22.	A
23.	A
24.	B
25.	B

TEST 2

DIRECTIONS: Each question or incomplete statement is followed by several suggested answers or completions. Select the one that BEST answers the question or completes the statement. *PRINT THE LETTER OF THE CORRECT ANSWER IN THE SPACE AT THE RIGHT.*

1. A foreman who is familiar with modern management principles should know that the one of the following requirements of an administrator which is LEAST important is his ability to
   A. coordinate work
   B. plan, organize, and direct the work under his control
   C. cooperate with others
   D. perform the duties of the employees under his jurisdiction

   1.____

2. When subordinates request his advice in solving problems encountered in their work, a certain chief occasionally answers the request by first asking the subordinate what he thinks should be done.
   This action by the chief is, on the whole,
   A. *desirable*, because it stimulates subordinates to give more thought to the solution of problems encountered
   B. *undesirable*, because it discourages subordinates from asking questions
   C. *desirable*, because it discourages subordinates from asking questions
   D. *undesirable*, because it undermines the confidence of subordinates in the ability of their supervisor

   2.____

3. Of the following factors that may be considered by a unit head in dealing with the tardy subordinate, the one which should be given LEAST consideration is the
   A. frequency with which the employee is tardy
   B. effect of the employee's tardiness upon the work of other employees
   C. willingness of the employee to work overtime when necessary
   D. cause of the employee's tardiness

   3.____

4. The MOST important requirement of a good inspectional report is that it should be
   A. properly addressed   B. lengthy
   C. clear and brief   D. spelled correctly

   4.____

5. Building superintendents frequently inquire about departmental inspectional procedures.
   Of the following, it is BEST to
   A. advise them to write to the department for an official reply
   B. refuse as the inspectional procedure is a restricted matter
   C. briefly explain the procedure to them
   D. avoid the inquiry by changing the subject

   5.____

6. Reprimanding a crew member before other workers is a
   A. *good* practice; the reprimand serves as a warning to the other workers
   B. *bad* practice; people usually resent criticism made in public
   C. *good* practice; the other workers will realize that the supervisor is fair
   D. *bad* practice; the other workers will take sides in the dispute

6.____

7. Of the following actions, the one which is LEAST likely to promote good work is for the group leader to
   A. praise workers for doing a good job
   B. call attention to the opportunities for promotion for better workers
   C. threaten to recommend discharge of workers who are below standard
   D. put into practice any good suggestion made by crew members

7.____

8. A supervisor notices that a member of his crew has skipped a routine step in his job.
   Of the following, the BEST action for the supervisor to take is to
   A. promptly question the worker about the incident
   B. immediately assign another man to complete the job
   C. bring up the incident the next time the worker asks for a favor
   D. say nothing about the incident but watch the worker carefully in the future

8.____

9. Assume you have been told to show a new worker how to operate a piece of equipment.
   Your FIRST step should be to
   A. ask the worker if he has any questions about the equipment
   B. permit the worker to operate the equipment himself while you carefully watch to prevent damage
   C. demonstrate the operation of the equipment for the worker
   D. have the worker read an instruction booklet on the maintenance of the equipment

9.____

10. Whenever a new man was assigned to his crew, the supervisor would introduce him to all other crew members, take him on a tour of the plant, tell him about bus schedules and places to eat.
    This practice is
    A. *good*; the new man is made to feel welcome
    B. *bad*; supervisors should not interfere in personal matters
    C. *good*; the new man knows that he can bring his personal problems to the supervisor
    D. *bad*; work time should not be spent on personal matters

10.____

11. The MOST important factor in successful leadership is the ability to
    A. obtain instant obedience to all orders
    B. establish friendly personal relations with crew members
    C. avoid disciplining crew members
    D. make crew members want to do what should be done

11.____

12. Explaining the reasons for departmental procedure to workers tends to
    A. waste time which should be used for productive purposes
    B. increase their interest in their work
    C. make them more critical of departmental procedures
    D. confuse them

13. If you want a job done well do it yourself.
    For a supervisor to follow this advice would be
    A. *good*; a supervisor is responsible for the work of his crew
    B. *bad*; a supervisor should train his men, not do their work
    C. *good*; a supervisor should be skilled in all jobs assigned to his crew
    D. *bad*; a supervisor loses respect when he works with his hands

14. When a supervisor discovers a mistake in one of the jobs for which his crew is responsible, it is MOST important for him to find out
    A. whether anybody else knows about the mistake
    B. who was to blame for the mistake
    C. how to prevent similar mistakes in the future
    D. whether similar mistakes occurred in the past

15. A supervisor who has to explain a new procedure to his crew should realize that questions from the crew USUALLY show that they
    A. are opposed to the new practice
    B. are completely confused by the explanation
    C. need more training in the new procedure
    D. are interested in the explanation

16. A good way for a supervisor to retain the confidence of his or her employees is to
    A. say as little as possible
    B. check work frequently
    C. make no promises unless they will be fulfilled
    D. never hesitate in giving an answer to any question

17. Good supervision is ESSENTIALLY a matter of
    A. patience in supervising workers   B. care in selecting workers
    C. skill in human relations   D. fairness in disciplining workers

18. It is MOST important for an employee who has been assigned a monotonous task to
    A. perform this task before doing other work
    B. ask another employee to help
    C. perform this task only after all other work has been completed
    D. take measures to prevent mistakes in performing the task

19. One of your employees has violated a minor agency regulation.
    The FIRST thing you should do is
    A. warn the employee that you will have to take disciplinary action if it should happen again
    B. ask the employee to explain his or her actions
    C. inform your supervisor and wait for advice
    D. write a memo describing the incident and place it in the employee's personnel file

20. One of your employees tells you that he feels you give him much more work than the other employees, and he is having trouble meeting your deadlines.
    You should
    A. ask if he has been under a lot of non-work related stress lately
    B. review his recent assignments to determine if he is correct
    C. explain that this is a busy time, but you are dividing the work equally
    D. tell him that he is the most competent employee and that is why he receives more work

21. A supervisor assigns one of his crew to complete a portion of a job. A short time later, the supervisor notices that the portion has not been completed.
    Of the following, the BEST way for the supervisor to handle this is to
    A. ask the crew member why he has not completed the assignment
    B. reprimand the crew member for not obeying orders
    C. assign another crew member to complete the assignment
    D. complete the assignment himself

22. Supposes that a member of your crew complains that you are *playing favorites* in assigning work.
    Of the following, the BEST method of handling the complaint is to
    A. deny it and refuse to discuss the matter with the worker
    B. take the opportunity to tell the worker what is wrong with his work
    C. ask the worker for examples to prove his point and try to clear up any misunderstanding
    D. promise to be more careful in making assignments in the future

23. A member of your crew comes to you with a complaint. After discussing the matter with him, it is clear that you have convinced him that his complaint was not justified.
    At this point, you should
    A. permit him to drop the matter
    B. make him admit his error
    C. pretend to see some justification in his complaint
    D. warn him against making unjustified complaints

24. Suppose that a supervisor has in his crew an older man who works rather slowly. In other respects, this man is a good worker; he is seldom absent, works carefully, never loafs, and is cooperative.

The BEST way for the supervisor to handle this worker is to
- A. try to get him to work faster and less carefully
- B. give him the most disagreeable job
- C. request that he be given special training
- D. permit him to work at his own speed

25. Suppose that a member of your crew comes to you with a suggestion he thinks will save time in doing a job. You realize immediately that it won't work.
Under these circumstances, your BEST action would be to
- A. thank the worker for the suggestion and forget about it
- B. explain to the worker why you think it won't work
- C. tell the worker to put the suggestion in writing
- D. ask the other members of your crew to criticize the suggestion

25.____

KEY (CORRECT ANSWERS)

1.	D		11.	D
2.	A		12.	B
3.	C		13.	B
4.	C		14.	C
5.	C		15.	D
6.	B		16.	C
7.	C		17.	C
8.	A		18.	D
9.	C		19.	B
10.	A		20.	B

21.	A
22.	C
23.	A
24.	D
25.	B

EXAMINATION SECTION
TEST 1

DIRECTIONS: Each question or incomplete statement is followed by several suggested answers or completions. Select the one that BEST answers the question or completes the statement. *PRINT THE LETTER OF THE CORRECT ANSWER IN THE SPACE AT THE RIGHT.*

1. When all of her employees are assigned to perform identical routine tasks, a supervisor would PROBABLY find it most difficult to differentiate among these employees as to the
   A. amount of work each completed
   B. initiative each one shows in doing the work
   C. number of errors in each one's work
   D. number of times each one is absent or late

2. The one of the following guiding principles to which a supervisor should give the GREATEST weight when it becomes necessary to discipline an employee is that the
   A. discipline should be of such a nature as to improve the future work of the employee
   B. main benefit gained in disciplining one employee is that all employees are kept from breaking the same rule
   C. morale of all the employees should be improved by the discipline of the one
   D. rules should be applied in a fixed and unchanging manner

3. In using praise to encourage employees to do better work, the supervisor should realize that praising an employee too often is not good MAINLY because the
   A. employee will be resented by her fellow employees
   B. employee will begin to think she's doing too much work
   C. praise will lose its value as an incentive
   D. supervisor doesn't have the time to praise an employee frequently

4. A supervisor notices that one of her best employees has apparently begun to loaf on the job.
   In this situation, the supervisor should FIRST
   A. allow the employee a period of grace in view of her excellent record
   B. change the employee's job assignment
   C. determine the reason for the change in the employee's behavior
   D. take disciplinary action immediately as she would with any other employee

5. A supervisor who wants to get a spirit of friendly cooperation from the employees in her unit is MOST likely to be successful if she
   A. makes no exceptions in strictly enforcing department procedures
   B. shows a cooperative spirit herself
   C. tells them they are the best in the department
   D. treats them to coffee once in a while

6. *Accidents do not just happen.*
   In view of this statement, it is important for the supervisor to realize that
   A. accidents are sometimes deliberate
   B. combinations of unavoidable circumstances cause accidents
   C. she must take the blame for each accident
   D. she should train her employees in accident prevention

6.____

7. Suppose your superior points out to you several jobs that were poorly done by the employees under your supervision.
   As the supervisor of these employees, you should
   A. accept responsibility for the poor work and take steps to improve the work in the future
   B. blame the employees for shirking on the job while you were busy on other work
   C. defend the employees since up to this time they were all good workers
   D. explain that the poor work was due to circumstances beyond your control

7.____

8. If a supervisor discovers a situation which is a possible source of grievance, it would be BEST for her to
   A. be ready to answer the employees when they make a direct complaint
   B. do nothing until the employees make a direct complaint
   C. tell the employees, in order to keep them from making a direct complaint, that nothing can be done
   D. try to remove the cause before the employees make a direct complaint

8.____

9. Suppose there is a departmental rule that requires supervisors to prepare reports of unusual incidents by the end of the tour of duty in which the incident occurs.
   The MAIN reason for requiring such prompt reporting is that
   A. a quick decision can be made whether the employee involved was neglectful of her duty
   B. other required reports cannot be made out until this one is turned in
   C. the facts are recorded before they are forgotten or confused by those involved in the incident
   D. the report is submitted before the supervisor required to make the report may possibly leave the department

9.____

10. A good practical method to use in determining whether an employee is doing his job properly is to
    A. assume that if he asks no questions, he knows the work
    B. question him directly on details of the job
    C. inspect and follow-up the work which is assigned to him
    D. ask other employees how this employee is making out

10.____

11. If an employee continually asks how he should do his work, you should
    A. dismiss him immediately
    B. pretend you do not hear him unless he persists
    C. explain the work carefully but encourage him to use his own judgment
    D. tell him not to ask so many questions

11.____

12. You have instructed an employee to complete a job in a certain area. To be sure that the employee understands the instructions you have given him, you should
    A. ask him to repeat the instructions to you
    B. check with him after he has done the job
    C. watch him while he is doing the job
    D. repeat the instructions to the employee

13. One of your men disagrees with your evaluation of his work. Of the following, the BEST way to handle this situation would be to
    A. explain that you are in a better position to evaluate his work than he is
    B. tell him that since other men are satisfied with your evaluation, he should accept their opinions
    C. explain the basis of your evaluation and discuss it with him
    D. refuse to discuss his complaint in order to maintain discipline

14. Of the following, the on which is NOT a quality of leadership desirable in a supervisor is
    A. intelligence   B. integrity   C. forcefulness   D. partiality

15. Of the following, the one which LEAST characterizes the grapevine is that it
    A. consists of a tremendous amount of rumor, conjecture, information, advice, prediction, and even orders.
    B. seems to rise spontaneously, is largely anonymous, spreads rapidly, and changes in unpredictable directions
    C. can be eliminated without any great effort
    D. commonly fills the gaps left by the regular organizational channels of communication

16. When a superintendent delegates authority to a foreman, of the following, it would be MOST advisable for the superintendent to
    A. set wide limits of such authority to allow the foreman considerable leeway
    B. define fairly closely the limits of the authority delegated to the foreman
    C. wait until the foreman has some experience in the assignment before setting limits to his authority
    D. inform him that it is the foreman's ultimate basic responsibility to get the work done

17. One of the hallmarks of a good supervisor is his ability to use many different methods of obtaining information about the status of work in progress. Which one of the following would probably indicate that a supervisor does NOT have this ability?
    A. Holding specified staff meetings at specified intervals
    B. Circulating among his subordinates as often as possible
    C. Holding staff meetings only when absolutely necessary
    D. Asking subordinates to come in and discuss the progress of their work and their problems

18. Of the following, the one which is the LEAST important factor in deciding that additional training is necessary for the men you supervise is that
    A. the quality of work is below standard
    B. supplies are being wasted
    C. too much time is required to do specific jobs
    D. the absentee rate has declined

19. To promote proper safety practices in the operation of power tools and equipment, you should emphasize in meetings with the staff that
    A. every accident can be prevented through proper safety regulations
    B. proper safety practices will probably make future safety meetings unnecessary
    C. when safety rules are followed, tools and equipment will work better
    D. safety rules are based on past experience with the best methods of preventing accidents

20. Employee morale is the way employees feel about each other and their job. To a supervisor, it should be a sign of good morale if the employees
    A. are late for work
    B. complain about their work
    C. willingly do difficult jobs
    D. take a long time to do simple jobs

21. A supervisor who encourages his workers to make suggestions about job improvement shows his workers that he
    A. is not smart enough to improve the job himself
    B. wants them to take part in making improvements
    C. does not take the job seriously
    D. is not a good supervisor

22. Suppose that your supervisor tells you that a procedure which has been followed for years is going to be changed. It is your job to make sure the workers you supervises understand and accept the new procedure.
    What would be the BEST thing for you to do in this situation?
    A. Give a copy of the new procedure to each worker with orders that it must be followed
    B. Explain the new procedure to one worker and have him explain it to the others
    C. Ask your supervisor to explain the new procedure since he has more authority
    D. call your workers together to explain and discuss the new procedure

23. One of the foundations of scientific management of an organization is the proper use of control measures.
    Of the following, the BEST way, in general, to implement control measures is to
    A. develop suitable procedures, systems, and guidelines for the organization
    B. evaluate the actual employees' job performance realistically and reasonably
    C. set standards which are designed to increase productivity
    D. publish a set of rules and insist upon strict compliance with these rules

24. A district superintendent would MOST likely be justified in taking up a matter with his borough superintendent when the problem involved
    A. a dispute among different factions in his district
    B. a section foreman's difficulties with his assistant foreman
    C. his own men and others not under his control
    D. methods of doing the work and the amount of production

25. The superintendent has the authority to recommend disciplinary action. He can BEST use this authority to
    A. demonstrate his authority as a superintendent
    B. improve a man's work
    C. make it less difficult for other superintendents to maintain order
    D. punish the men for wrong-doing

KEY (CORRECT ANSWERS)

1.	B		11.	C
2.	A		12.	A
3.	C		13.	C
4.	C		14.	D
5.	B		15.	C
6.	D		16.	B
7.	A		17.	C
8.	D		18.	D
9.	C		19.	D
10.	C		20.	C

21.	B
22.	D
23.	C
24.	B
25.	B

TEST 2

DIRECTIONS: Each question or incomplete statement is followed by several suggested answers or completions. Select the one that BEST answers the question or completes the statement. *PRINT THE LETTER OF THE CORRECT ANSWER IN THE SPACE AT THE RIGHT.*

1. From the standpoint of equal opportunity, the MOST critical item that a superintendent should focus on is
    A. assigning only minority workers to supervisory positions
    B. helping minority employees to upgrade their knowledge so they may qualify for higher positions
    C. placing minority workers in job categories above their present level of ability so that they can *sink or swim*
    D. disregarding merit system principles

   1.____

2. After careful deliberation, you have decided that one of your workers should be disciplined.
   It is MOST important that the
    A. discipline be severe for best results
    B. discipline be delayed as long as possible
    C. worker understands why he is being disciplined
    D. other workers be consulted before the discipline is administered

   2.____

3. Of the following, the MOST important qualities of an employee chosen for a supervisory position are
    A. education and intelligence
    B. interest in the objectives and activities of the agency
    C. skill in performing the type of work to be supervised
    D. knowledge of the work and leadership ability

   3.____

4. Of the following, the CHIEF characteristic which distinguishes a good supervisor from a poor supervisor is the good supervisor's
    A. ability to favorably impress others
    B. unwillingness to accept monotony or routine
    C. ability to deal constructively with problem situations
    D. strong drive to overcome opposition

   4.____

5. Of the following, the MAIN disadvantage of on-the-job training is that, generally,
    A. special equipment may be needed
    B. production may be slowed down
    C. the instructor must maintain an individual relationship with the trainee
    D. the on-the-job instructor must be better qualified than the classroom instructor

   5.____

6. If it becomes necessary for you, as a supervisor, to give a subordinate employee confidential information, the MOST effective of the following steps to take is to make sure the information is kept confidential by the employee is to

   6.____

A. tell the employee that the information is confidential and is not to be repeated
B. threaten the employee with disciplinary action if the information is repeated
C. offer the employee a merit increase as an incentive for keeping the information confidential
D. remind the employee at least twice a day that the information is confidential and is not to be repeated

7. Three new men have just been assigned to work under your supervision. Every time you give them an assignment, one of these men asks you several questions.
Of the following, the MOST desirable action for you to take is to
    A. assure him of your confidence in his ability to carry out the assignment correctly without asking so many questions
    B. have all three men listen to your answers to these questions
    C. point out that the other two men do the job without asking so many questions
    D. tell him to see if he can get the answers from other workers before coming to you

8. Two of your subordinates suggest that you recommend a third man for an above-standard service rating because of his superior work.
You should
    A. ask the two subordinates whether the third man knows that they intended to discuss this matter with you
    B. explain to the two subordinates that an above-standard service rating for one man would have a detrimental effect on many of the other men
    C. recommend the man for an above-standard service rating if there is sufficient justification for it
    D. tell the two subordinates that the matter of service ratings is not their concern

9. All of the following are indications of good employee morale EXCEPT
    A. the number of grievances are lowered
    B. labor turnover is decreased
    C. the amount of supervision required is lowered
    D. levels of production are lowered

10. All of the following statements regarding the issuance of direct orders are true EXCEPT
    A. use direct orders only when necessary
    B. make sure that the receiver of the direct order is qualified to carry out the order
    C. issue direct orders in clear, concise words
    D. give direct orders only in writing

11. In order to achieve the BEST results in on-the-job training, supervisors should
    A. allow frequent coffee breaks during the training period
    B. be in a higher salary range than that of the individuals they are training
    C. have had instructions or experience in conducting such training
    D. have had a minimum of five years' experience in the job

    11.____

12. Of the following, the LEAST important quality of a good supervisor is
    A. technical competence
    B. teaching ability
    C. ability to communicate with others
    D. ability to socialize with subordinates

    12.____

13. One of your usually very hard working, reliable employees brings in a bottle of whiskey to celebrate his birthday during the rest period.
    Which one of the following actions should you take?
    A. Offer to pay for the cost of the whiskey
    B. Confiscate the bottle
    C. Tell him to celebrate after working hours
    D. Pretend that you have not seen the bottle of whiskey

    13.____

14. Assume that you find it necessary to discipline two subordinates, Mr. Tate and Mr. Sawyer, for coming to work late on several occasions. Their latenesses have had disruptive effects on the work schedule, and you have given both of them several verbal warnings. Mr. Tate has been in your work unit for many years, and his work has always been satisfactory. Mr. Sawyer is a probationary employee, who has had some problem in learning your procedures. You decide to give Mr. Tate one more warning, in private, for his latenesses.
    According to good supervisory practice, which one of the following disciplinary actions should you take with regard to Mr. Sawyer?
    A. Give him a reprimand in front of his co-workers, to make a lasting impression
    B. Recommend dismissal since he has not yet completed his probationary period
    C. Give him one more warning, in private, for his latenesses
    D. Recommend a short suspension or payroll deduction to impress upon him the importance of coming to work on time

    14.____

15. Assume that you have delegated a very important work assignment to Johnson, one of your most experienced subordinates. Prior to completion of the assignment, your superior accidentally discovers that the assignment is being carried out incorrectly, and tells you about it.
    Which one of the following responses is MOST appropriate for you to give to your superior?
    A. *I take full responsibility, and I will see to it that the assignment is carried out correctly.*
    B. *Johnson has been with us for many years now and should know better.*

    15.____

C. *It really isn't Johnson's fault, rather it is the fault of the ancient equipment we have to do the job.*
D. *I think you should inform Johnson since he is the one at fault, not I.*

16. Assume that you observe that one of your employees is talking excessively with other employees, quitting early, and taking unusually long rest periods. Despite these abuses, she is one of your most productive employees, and her work is usually of the highest quality.
    Of the following, the MOST appropriate action to take with regard to this employee is to
    A. ignore these infractions since she is one of your best workers
    B. ask your superior to reprimand her so that you can remain on the employee's good side
    C. reprimand her since not doing so would lower the morale of the other employees
    D. ask another of your subordinates to mention these infractions to the offending employee and suggest that she stop breaking rules

16.____

17. Assume that you have noticed that an employee whose attendance had been quite satisfactory is now showing marked evidence of a consistent pattern of absences.
    Of the following, the BEST way to cope with this problem is to
    A. wait several weeks to see whether this pattern continues
    B. meet with the employee to try to find out the reasons for this change
    C. call a staff meeting and discuss the need for good attendance
    D. write a carefully worded warning to the employee

17.____

18. It is generally agreed that the successful supervisor must know how to wisely delegate work to her subordinates since she cannot do everything herself. Which one of the following practices is MOST likely to result in ineffective delegation by a supervisor?
    A. Establishment of broad controls to assure feedback about any deviations from plans
    B. Willingness to let subordinates use their own ideas about how to get the job done, where appropriate
    C. Constant observance of employees to see if they are making any mistakes
    D. Granting of enough authority to make possible the accomplishment of the delegated work

18.____

19. Suppose that, in accordance with grievance procedures, an employee brings a complaint to you, his immediate supervisor.
    In dealing with his complaint, the one of the following which is MOST important for you to do is to
    A. talk to the employee's co-workers to learn whether the complaint is justified
    B. calm the employee by assuring him that you will look into the matter as soon as possible

19.____

C. tell your immediate superior about the employee's complaint
D. give the employee an opportunity to tell the full story

20. Holding staff meetings at regular intervals is generally considered to be a good supervisory practice.
    Which one of the following subjects is LEAST desirable for discussion at such a meeting?
    A. Revisions in agency personnel policies
    B. Violation of an agency rule by one of the employees present
    C. Problems of waste and breakage in the work area
    D. Complaints of employees about working conditions

21. Suppose that you are informed that your staff is soon to be reduced by one-third due to budget problems.
    Which one of the following steps would be LEAST advisable in your effort to maintain a quality service with the smaller number of employees?
    A. Directing employees to speed up operations
    B. Giving employees training or retraining
    C. Rearranging the work area
    D. Revising work methods

22. Of the following which action on the part of the supervisor LEAST likely to contribute to upgrading the skills of her subordinates?
    A. Providing appropriate training to subordinates
    B. Making periodic evaluations of subordinates and discussing the evaluations with the subordinates
    C. Consistently assigning subordinates to those tasks with which they are familiar
    D. Giving increased responsibility to appropriate subordinates

23. Suppose that a new employee on your staff has difficulty in performing his assigned tasks after having been given training.
    Of the following courses of action, the one which would be BEST for you, his supervisor, to take FIRST is to
    A. change his work assignment
    B. give him a poor evaluation since he is obviously unable to do the work
    C. give him the training again
    D. have him work with an employee who is more experienced in the tasks for a short while

24. Several times, an employee has reported to work unit for duty because he had been drinking. He refused to get counseling for his emotional problems when this was suggested by his superior. Last week, his supervisor warned him that he would face disciplinary action if he again reported to work unfit for duty because of drinking. Now, the employee has again reported to work in that condition.

Of the following, the BEST action for the supervisor to take now would be to
A. arrange to have the employee transferred to another work location
B. give the employee one more chance by pretending to not notice his condition this time
C. start disciplinary action against the employee
D. warn him that he will face disciplinary action if he reports for work in that condition again

25. An employee has been calling in sick repeatedly, and these absences have disrupted the work schedule.
To try to make sure that the employee use sick leave only on days when he is actually sick, which of the following actions would be the BEST for his supervisor to take?
A. Telephone the employee's home on days when he is out on sick leave
B. Require the employee to obtain a note from a physician explaining the reason for his absence whenever he uses sick leave in the future
C. Require that he get a complete physical examination and have his doctor send a report to the supervisor
D. Warn the employee that he will face disciplinary action the next time he stays out on sick leave

25.____

KEY (CORRECT ANSWERS)

1. B
2. C
3. D
4. C
5. B

6. A
7. B
8. C
9. D
10. D

11. C
12. D
13. C
14. C
15. A

16. C
17. B
18. C
19. D
20. B

21. A
22. C
23. D
24. C
25. B

TEST 3

DIRECTIONS: Each question or incomplete statement is followed by several suggested answers or completions. Select the one that BEST answers the question or completes the statement. *PRINT THE LETTER OF THE CORRECT ANSWER IN THE SPACE AT THE RIGHT.*

1. Suppose that, as a supervisor, you have an idea for changing the way a certain task is performed by your staff so that it will be less tedious and get done faster. Of the following, the MOST advisable action for you to take regarding this idea is to
   A. issue a written memorandum explaining the new method and giving reasons why it is to replace the old one
   B. discuss it with your staff to get their reactions and suggestions
   C. set up a training class in the new method for your staff
   D. try it out on an experimental basis on half the staff

   1.____

2. A troubled subordinate privately approaches his supervisor in order to talk about a problem on the job.
   In this situation, the one of the following actions that is NOT desirable on the part of the supervisor is to
   A. ask the subordinate pertinent questions to help develop points further
   B. close his office door during the talk to block noisy distractions
   C. allow sufficient time to complete the discussion with the subordinate
   D. take over the conversation so the employee won't be embarrassed

   2.____

3. Suppose that one of your goals as a supervisor is to foster good working relationships between yourself and your employees, without undermining your supervisory effectiveness by being too friendly.
   Of the following, the BEST way to achieve this goal when dealing with employees' work problems is to
   A. discourage individual personal conferences by using regularly scheduled staff meetings to discuss work problems
   B. try to resolve work problems within a relatively short period of time
   C. insist that employees put all work problems into writing before seeing you
   D. maintain an open-door policy, allowing employees complete freedom of access to you without making appointments to discuss work problems

   3.____

4. An employee under your supervision complains that he is assigned to work late more often than any of the other employees. You check the records and find that this isn't so.
   You should
   A. advise this employee not to worry about what the other employees do but to see that he puts in a full day's work himself
   B. explain to this employee that you get the same complaint from all the other employees
   C. inform this employee that you have checked the records and the complaint is not justified
   D. not assign this employee to work late for a few days in order to keep him satisfied

   4.____

92

5. An employee has reported late for work several times.
   His supervisor should
   A. give this employee less desirable assignments
   B. overlook the lateness if the employee's work is otherwise exceptional
   C. recommend disciplinary action for habitual lateness
   D. talk the matter over with the employee before doing anything further

6. In choosing a man to be in charge in his absence, the supervisor should select FIRST the employee who
   A. has ability to supervise others
   B. has been longest with the organization
   C. has the nicest appearance and manner
   D. is most skilled in his assigned duties

7. An employee under your supervision comes to you to complain about a decision you have made in assigning the men. He is excited and angry. You think what he is complaining about is not important, but it seems very important to him.
   The BEST way for you to handle this is to
   A. let him talk until *he gets it off his chest* and then explain the reasons for your decision
   B. refuse to talk to him until he has cooled off
   C. show him at once how unimportant the matter is and how ridiculous his arguments are
   D. tell him to take it up with your superior if he disagrees with your decision

8. Suppose that a new employee has been appointed and assigned to your supervision.
   When this man reports for work, it would be BEST for you to
   A. ask him questions about different problems connected with his line of work and see if he answers them correctly
   B. check him carefully while he carries out some routine assignment that you give him
   C. explain to him the general nature of the work he will be required to do
   D. make a careful study of his previous work record before coming to your department

9. *The competent supervisor will be friendly with the employees under his supervision but will avoid close familiarity.*
   This statement is justified MAINLY because
   A. a friendly attitude on the part of the supervisor toward the employee is likely to cause suspicion on the part of the employee
   B. a supervisor can handle his employees better if he doesn't know their personal problems
   C. close familiarity may interfere with the discipline needed for good supervisor-subordinate relationships
   D. familiarity with the employees may be a sign of lack of ability on the part of the supervisor

10. An employee disagrees with the instructions that you, his supervisor, have given him for carrying out a certain assignment.
    The BEST action for you to take is to tell this employee that
    A. he can do what he wants but you will hold him responsible for failure
    B. orders must be carried out or morale will fall apart
    C. this job has been done in this way for many years with great success
    D. you will be glad to listen to his objections and to his suggestions for improvement

11. As a supervisor, it is LEAST important for you to use a new employee's probationary period for the purpose of
    A. carefully checking how he performs the work you assign him
    B. determining whether he can perform the duties of his job efficiently
    C. preparing him for promotion to a higher position
    D. showing him how to carry out his assigned duties properly

12. Suppose you have just given an employee under your supervision instructions on how to carry out a certain assignment.
    The BEST way to check that he has understood your instructions is to
    A. ask him to repeat your instructions word for word
    B. check the progress of his work the first chance you get
    C. invite him to ask questions if he has any doubts
    D. question him briefly about the main points of the assignment

13. Suppose you find it necessary to change a procedure that the men under your supervision have been following for a long time.
    A good way to get their cooperation for this change would be to
    A. bring them together to talk over the new procedure and explain the reasons for its adoption
    B. explain to the men that if most of them still don't approve of the change after giving it a fair try you will consider giving it up
    C. give them a few weeks' notice of the proposed change in procedure
    D. not enforce the new procedure strictly at the beginning

14. An order can be given by a supervisor in such a way as to make the employee want to obey it.
    According to this statement, it is MOST reasonable to suppose that
    A. a person will be glad to obey an order if he realizes that he must
    B. if an order is given properly, it will be obeyed more willingly
    C. it is easier to obey an order than to give one correctly
    D. supervisors should inspire confidence by their actions as well as by their words

15. If one of the men you supervise disagrees with how you rate his work, the BEST way for you to handle this is to
    A. advise him to appeal to your superior about it
    B. decline to discuss the matter with him in order to keep discipline
    C. explain why you rate him the way you do and talk it over with him
    D. tell him that you are better qualified to rate his work than he is

16. A supervisor should be familiar with the experience and abilities of the employees under his supervision MAINLY because
    A. each employee's work is highly important and requires a person of outstanding ability
    B. it will help him to know which employees are best fitted for certain assignments
    C. nearly all men have the same basic ability to do any job equally well
    D. superior background shortly shows itself in superior work quality, regardless of assignment

17. The competent supervisor will try to develop respect rather than fear in his subordinates.
    This statement is justified MAINLY because
    A. fear is always present and, for best results, respect must be developed to offset it
    B. it is generally easier to develop respect in the men than it is to develop fear
    C. men who respect their supervisor are more likely to give more than the required minimum amount and quality of work
    D. respect is based on the individual, and fear is based on the organization as a whole

18. If one of the employees you supervise does outstanding work, you should
    A. explain to him how his work can still be improved so that he will not become self-satisfied
    B. mildly criticize the other men for not doing as good a job as this man
    C. praise him for his work so that he will know it is appreciated
    D. say nothing or he might become conceited

19. A supervisor can BEST help establish good morale among his employees if he
    A. confides in them about his personal problems in order to encourage them to confide in him
    B. encourages them to become friendly with him but discourages social engagements with them
    C. points out to them the advantages of having a cooperative spirit in the department
    D. sticks to the same rules that he expects them to follow

20. The one of the following situations which would seem to indicate poor scheduling of work by the supervisor is
    A. everybody seeming to be very busy at the same time
    B. re-assignment of a man to other work because of breakdown of a piece of equipment
    C. two employees on vacation at the same time
    D. two operators waiting to use the same equipment at the same time

KEY (CORRECT ANSWERS)

1.	B	11.	C
2.	D	12.	D
3.	B	13.	A
4.	C	14.	B
5.	D	15.	C
6.	A	16.	B
7.	A	17.	C
8.	C	18.	C
9.	C	19.	D
10.	D	20.	D

PHILOSOPHY, PRINCIPLES, PRACTICES, AND TECHNICS OF SUPERVISION, ADMINISTRATION, MANAGEMENT, AND ORGANIZATION

TABLE OF CONTENTS

	Page
MEANING OF SUPERVISION	1
THE OLD AND THE NEW SUPERVISION	1
THE EIGHT (8) BASIC PRINCIPLES OF THE NEW SUPERVISION	1
I. Principle of Responsibility	1
II. Principle of Authority	2
III. Principle of Self-Growth	2
IV. Principle of Individual Worth	2
V. Principle of Creative Leadership	2
VI. Principle of Success and Failure	2
VII. Principle of Science	3
VIII. Principle of Cooperation	3
WHAT IS ADMINISTRATION?	3
I. Practices Commonly Classed as "Supervisory"	3
II. Practices Commonly Classed as "Administrative"	3
III. Practices Commonly Classed as Both "Supervisory" and "Administrative"	4
RESPONSIBILITIES OF THE SUPERVISOR	4
COMPETENCIES OF THE SUPERVISOR	4
THE PROFESSIONAL SUPERVISOR-EMPLOYEE RELATIONSHIP	4
MINI-TEXT IN SUPERVISION, ADMINISTRATION, MANAGEMENT, AND ORGANIZATION	5
I. Brief Highlights	5
A. Levels of Management	6
B. What the Supervisor Must Learn	6
C. A Definition of Supervision	6
D. Elements of the Team Concept	6
E. Principles of Organization	6
F. The Four Important Parts of Every Job	7
G. Principles of Delegation	7
H. Principles of Effective Communications	7
I. Principles of Work Improvement	7
J. Areas of Job Improvement	7
K. Seven Key Points in Making Improvements	8

	L.	Corrective Techniques for Job Improvement	8
	M.	A Planning Checklist	8
	N.	Five Characteristics of Good Directions	9
	O.	Types of Directions	9
	P.	Controls	9
	Q.	Orienting the New Employee	9
	R.	Checklist for Orienting New Employees	9
	S.	Principles of Learning	10
	T.	Causes of Poor Performance	10
	U.	Four Major Steps in On-the-Job Instructions	10
	V.	Employees Want Five Things	10
	W.	Some Don'ts in Regard to Praise	11
	X.	How to Gain Your Workers' Confidence	11
	Y.	Sources of Employee Problems	11
	Z.	The Supervisor's Key to Discipline	11
	AA.	Five Important Processes of Management	12
	BB.	When the Supervisor Fails to Plan	12
	CC.	Fourteen General Principles of Management	12
	DD.	Change	12

II. Brief Topical Summaries — 13
    A. Who/What is the Supervisor? — 13
    B. The Sociology of Work — 13
    C. Principles and Practices of Supervision — 14
    D. Dynamic Leadership — 14
    E. Processes for Solving Problems — 15
    F. Training for Results — 15
    G. Health, Safety, and Accident Prevention — 16
    H. Equal Employment Opportunity — 16
    I. Improving Communications — 16
    J. Self-Development — 17
    K. Teaching and Training — 17
        1. The Teaching Process — 17
            a. Preparation — 17
            b. Presentation — 18
            c. Summary — 18
            d. Application — 18
            e. Evaluation — 18
        2. Teaching Methods — 18
            a. Lecture — 18
            b. Discussion — 18
            c. Demonstration — 19
            d. Performance — 19
            e. Which Method to Use — 19

PHILOSOPHY, PRINCIPLES, PRACTICES, AND TECHNICS
OF
SUPERVISION, ADMINISTRATION, MANAGEMENT, AND ORGANIZATION

MEANING OF SUPERVISION

The extension of the democratic philosophy has been accompanied by an extension in the scope of supervision. Modern leaders and supervisors no longer think of supervision in the narrow sense of being confined chiefly to visiting employees, supplying materials, or rating the staff. They regard supervision as being intimately related to all the concerned agencies of society, they speak of the supervisor's function in terms of "growth," rather than the "improvement" of employees.

This modern concept of supervision may be defined as follows: Supervision is leadership and the development of leadership within groups which are cooperatively engaged in inspection, research, training, guidance, and evaluation.

THE OLD AND THE NEW SUPERVISION

TRADITIONAL
1. Inspection
2. Focused on the employee
3. Visitation
4. Random and haphazard
5. Imposed and authoritarian
6. One person usually

MODERN
1. Study and analysis
2. Focused on aims, materials, methods, supervisors, employees, environment
3. Demonstrations, intervisitation, workshops, directed reading, bulletins, etc.
4. Definitely organized and planned (scientific)
5. Cooperative and democratic
6. Many persons involved (creative)

THE EIGHT (8) BASIC PRINCIPLES OF THE NEW SUPERVISION

I. Principle of Responsibility
   Authority to act and responsibility for acting must be joined.
   A. If you give responsibility, give authority.
   B. Define employee duties clearly.
   C. Protect employees from criticism by others.
   D. Recognize the rights as well as obligations of employees.
   E. Achieve the aims of a democratic society insofar as it is possible within the area of your work.
   F. Establish a situation favorable to training and learning.
   G. Accept ultimate responsibility for everything done in your section, unit, office, division, department.
   H. Good administration and good supervision are inseparable.

II. Principle of Authority
The success of the supervisor is measured by the extent to which the power of authority is not used.
   A. Exercise simplicity and informality in supervision
   B. Use the simplest machinery of supervision
   C. If it is good for the organization as a whole, it is probably justified.
   D. Seldom be arbitrary or authoritative.
   E. Do not base your work on the power of position or of personality.
   F. Permit and encourage the free expression of opinions.

III. Principle of Self-Growth
The success of the supervisor is measured by the extent to which, and the speed with which, he is no longer needed.
   A. Base criticism on principles, not on specifics.
   B. Point out higher activities to employees.
   C. Train for self-thinking by employees to meet new situations.
   D. Stimulate initiative, self-reliance, and individual responsibility
   E. Concentrate on stimulating the growth of employees rather than on removing defects.

IV. Principle of Individual Worth
Respect for the individual is a paramount consideration in supervision.
   A. Be human and sympathetic in dealing with employees.
   B. Don't nag about things to be done.
   C. Recognize the individual differences among employees and seek opportunities to permit best expression of each personality.

V. Principle of Creative Leadership
The best supervision is that which is not apparent to the employee.
   A. Stimulate, don't drive employees to creative action.
   B. Emphasize doing good things.
   C. Encourage employees to do what they do best.
   D. Do not be too greatly concerned with details of subject or method.
   E. Do not be concerned exclusively with immediate problems and activities.
   F. Reveal higher activities and make them both desired and maximally possible.
   G. Determine procedures in the light of each situation but see that these are derived from a sound basic philosophy.
   H. Aid, inspire, and lead so as to liberate the creative spirit latent in all good employees.

VI. Principle of Success and Failure
There are no unsuccessful employees, only unsuccessful supervisors who have failed to give proper leadership.
   A. Adapt suggestions to the capacities, attitudes, and prejudices of employees.
   B. Be gradual, be progressive, be persistent.
   C. Help the employee find the general principle; have the employee apply his own problem to the general principle.
   D. Give adequate appreciation for good work and honest effort.
   E. Anticipate employee difficulties and help to prevent them.
   F. Encourage employees to do the desirable things they will do anyway.
   G. Judge your supervision by the results it secures.

VII. Principle of Science
Successful supervision is scientific, objective, and experimental. It is based on facts, not on prejudices.
   A. Be cumulative in results.
   B. Never divorce your suggestions from the goals of training.
   C. Don't be impatient of results.
   D. Keep all matters on a professional, not a personal, level.
   E. Do not be concerned exclusively with immediate problems and activities.
   F. Use objective means of determining achievement and rating where possible.

VIII. Principle of Cooperation
Supervision is a cooperative enterprise between supervisor and employee.
   A. Begin with conditions as they are.
   B. Ask opinions of all involved when formulating policies.
   C. Organization is as good as its weakest link.
   D. Let employees help to determine policies and department programs.
   E. Be approachable and accessible—physically and mentally.
   F. Develop pleasant social relationships.

WHAT IS ADMINISTRATION

Administration is concerned with providing the environment, the material facilities, and the operational procedures that will promote the maximum growth and development of supervisors and employees. (Organization is an aspect and a concomitant of administration.)

There is no sharp line of demarcation between supervision and administration; these functions are intimately interrelated and, often, overlapping. They are complementary activities.

I. Practices Commonly Classed as "Supervisory"
   A. Conducting employees' conferences
   B. Visiting sections, units, offices, divisions, departments
   C. Arranging for demonstrations
   D. Examining plans
   E. Suggesting professional reading
   F. Interpreting bulletins
   G. Recommending in-service training courses
   H. Encouraging experimentation
   I. Appraising employee morale
   J. Providing for intervisitation

II. Practices Commonly Classified as "Administrative"
   A. Management of the office
   B. Arrangement of schedules for extra duties
   C. Assignment of rooms or areas
   D. Distribution of supplies
   E. Keeping records and reports
   F. Care of audio-visual materials
   G. Keeping inventory records
   H. Checking record cards and books

    I.   Programming special activities
    J.   Checking on the attendance and punctuality of employees

III. Practices Commonly Classified as Both "Supervisory" and "Administrative"
    A.   Program construction
    B.   Testing or evaluating outcomes
    C.   Personnel accounting
    D.   Ordering instructional materials

RESPONSIBILITIES OF THE SUPERVISOR

A person employed in a supervisory capacity must constantly be able to improve his own efficiency and ability. He represent the employer to the employees and only continuous self-examination can make him a capable supervisor.

Leadership and training are the supervisor's responsibility. An efficient working unit is one in which the employees work with the supervisor. It is his job to bring out the best in his employees. He must always be relaxed, courteous, and calm in his association with his employees. Their feelings are important, and a harsh attitude does not develop the most efficient employees.

COMPETENCES OF THE SUPERVISOR

   I.   Complete knowledge of the duties and responsibilities of his position.
   II. To be able to organize a job, plan ahead, and carry through.
   III. To have self-confidence and initiative.
   IV. To be able to handle the unexpected situation and make quick decisions.
   V.   To be able to properly train subordinates in the positions they are best suited for.
   VI. To be able to keep good human relations among his subordinates.
   VII. To be able to keep good human relations between his subordinates and himself and to earn their respect and trust.

THE PROFESSIONAL SUPERVISOR-EMPLOYEE RELATIONSHIP

There are two kinds of efficiency: one kind is only apparent and is produced in organizations through the exercise of mere discipline; this is but a simulation of the second, or true, efficiency which springs from spontaneous cooperation. If you are a manager, no matter how great or small your responsibility, it is your job, in the final analysis, to create and develop this involuntary cooperation among the people whom you supervise. For, no matter how powerful a combination of money, machines, and materials a company may have, this is a dead and sterile thing without a team of willing, thinking, and articulate people to guide it.

The following 21 points are presented as indicative of the exemplary basic relationship that should exist between supervisor and employee:

1. Each person wants to be liked and respected by his fellow employee and wants to be treated with consideration and respect by his superior.
2. The most competent employee will make an error. However, in a unit where good relations exist between the supervisor and his employees, tenseness and fear do not exist. Thus, errors are not hidden or covered up, and the efficiency of a unit is not impaired.

3. Subordinates resent rules, regulations, or orders that are unreasonable or unexplained.
4. Subordinates are quick to resent unfairness, harshness, injustices, and favoritism.
5. An employee will accept responsibility if he knows that he will be complimented for a job well done, and not too harshly chastised for failure; that his supervisor will check the cause of the failure, and, if it was the supervisor's fault, he will assume the blame therefore. If it was the employee's fault, his supervisor will explain the correct method or means of handling the responsibility.
6. An employee wants to receive credit for a suggestion he has made, that is used. If a suggestion cannot be used, the employee is entitled to an explanation. The supervisor should not say "no" and close the subject.
7. Fear and worry slow up a worker's ability. Poor working environment can impair his physical and mental health. A good supervisor avoids forceful methods, threats, and arguments to get a job done.
8. A forceful supervisor is able to train his employees individually and as a team, and is able to motivate them in the proper channels.
9. A mature supervisor is able to properly evaluate his subordinates and to keep them happy and satisfied.
10. A sensitive supervisor will never patronize his subordinates.
11. A worthy supervisor will respect his employees' confidences.
12. Definite and clear-cut responsibilities should be assigned to each executive.
13. Responsibility should always be coupled with corresponding authority.
14. No change should be made in the scope or responsibilities of a position without a definite understanding to that effect on the part of all persons concerned.
15. No executive or employee, occupying a single position in the organization, should be subject to definite orders from more than one source.
16. Orders should never be given to subordinates over the head of a responsible executive. Rather than do this, the officer in question should be supplanted.
17. Criticisms of subordinates should, whoever possible, be made privately, and in no case should a subordinate be criticized in the presence of executives or employees of equal or lower rank.
18. No dispute or difference between executives or employees as to authority or responsibilities should be considered too trivial for prompt and careful adjudication.
19. Promotions, wage changes, and disciplinary action should always be approved by the executive immediately superior to the one directly responsible.
20. No executive or employee should ever be required, or expected, to be at the same time an assistant to, and critic of, another.
21. Any executive whose work is subject to regular inspection should, wherever practicable, be given the assistance and facilities necessary to enable him to maintain an independent check of the quality of his work.

MINI-TEXT IN SUPERVISION, ADMINISTRATION, MANAGEMENT, AND ORGANIZATION

I. Brief Highlights

Listed concisely and sequentially are major headings and important data in the field for quick recall and review.

A. Levels of Management
Any organization of some size has several levels of management. In terms of a ladder, the levels are:

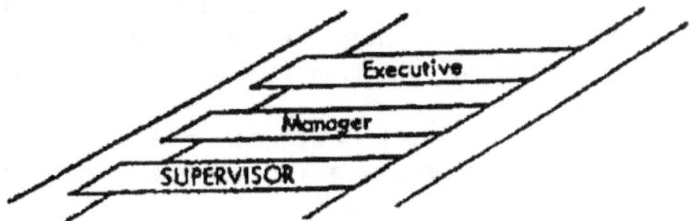

The first level is very important because it is the beginning point of management leadership.

B. What the Supervisor Must Learn
A supervisor must learn to:
1. Deal with people and their differences
2. Get the job done through people
3. Recognize the problems when they exist
4. Overcome obstacles to good performance
5. Evaluate the performance of people
6. Check his own performance in terms of accomplishment

C. A Definition of Supervisor
The term supervisor means any individual having authority, in the interests of the employer, to hire, transfer, suspend, lay-off, recall, promote, discharge, assign, reward, or discipline other employees or responsibility to direct them, or to adjust their grievances, or effectively to recommend such action, if, in connection with the foregoing, exercise of such authority is not of a merely routine or clerical nature but requires the use of independent judgment.

D. Elements of the Team Concept
What is involved in teamwork? The component parts are:
1. Members
2. A leader
3. Goals
4. Plans
5. Cooperation
6. Spirit

E. Principles of Organization
1. A team member must know what his job is.
2. Be sure that the nature and scope of a job are understood.
3. Authority and responsibility should be carefully spelled out.
4. A supervisor should be permitted to make the maximum number of decisions affecting his employees.
5. Employees should report to only one supervisor.
6. A supervisor should direct only as many employees as he can handle effectively.
7. An organization plan should be flexible.

8. Inspection and performance of work should be separate.
9. Organizational problems should receive immediate attention.
10. Assign work in line with ability and experience.

F. The Four Important Parts of Every Job
1. Inherent in every job is the *accountability* for results.
2. A second set of factors in every job is *responsibilities*.
3. Along with duties and responsibilities one must have the *authority* to act within certain limits without obtaining permission to proceed.
4. No job exists in a vacuum. The supervisor is surrounded by key *relationships*.

G. Principles of Delegation
Where work is delegated for the first time, the supervisor should think in terms of these questions:
1. Who is best qualified to do this?
2. Can an employee improve his abilities by doing this?
3. How long should an employee spend on this?
4. Are there any special problems for which he will need guidance?
5. How broad a delegation can I make?

H. Principles of Effective Communications
1. Determine the media.
2. To whom directed?
3. Identification and source authority.
4. Is communication understood?

I. Principles of Work Improvement
1. Most people usually do only the work which is assigned to them.
2. Workers are likely to fit assigned work into the time available to perform it.
3. A good workload usually stimulates output.
4. People usually do their best work when they know that results will be reviewed or inspected.
5. Employees usually feel that someone else is responsible for conditions of work, workplace layout, job methods, type of tools/equipment, and other such factors.
6. Employees are usually defensive about their job security.
7. Employees have natural resistance to change.
8. Employees can support or destroy a supervisor.
9. A supervisor usually earns the respect of his people through his personal example of diligence and efficiency.

J. Areas of Job Improvement
The areas of job improvement are quite numerous, but the most common ones which a supervisor can identify and utilize are:
1. Departmental layout
2. Flow of work
3. Workplace layout
4. Utilization of manpower
5. Work methods
6. Materials handling

7. Utilization
8. Motion economy

K. Seven Key Points in Making Improvements
   1. Select the job to be improved
   2. Study how it is being done now
   3. Question the present method
   4. Determine actions to be taken
   5. Chart proposed method
   6. Get approval and apply
   7. Solicit worker participation

L. Corrective Techniques of Job Improvement
   Specific Problems
   1. Size of workload
   2. Inability to meet schedules
   3. Strain and fatigue
   4. Improper use of men and skills
   5. Waste, poor quality, unsafe conditions
   6. Bottleneck conditions that hinder output
   7. Poor utilization of equipment and machine
   8. Efficiency and productivity of labor

   General Improvement
   1. Departmental layout
   2. Flow of work
   3. Work plan layout
   4. Utilization of manpower
   5. Work methods
   6. Materials handling
   7. Utilization of equipment
   8. Motion economy

   Corrective Techniques
   1. Study with scale model
   2. Flow chart study
   3. Motion analysis
   4. Comparison of units produced to standard allowance
   5. Methods analysis
   6. Flow chart and equipment study
   7. Down time vs. running time
   8. Motion analysis

M. A Planning Checklist
   1. Objectives
   2. Controls
   3. Delegations
   4. Communications
   5. Resources
   6. Manpower

7. Equipment
8. Supplies and materials
9. Utilization of time
10. Safety
11. Money
12. Work
13. Timing of improvements

N. Five Characteristics of Good Directions
In order to get results, directions must be:
1. Possible of accomplishment
2. Agreeable with worker interests
3. Related to mission
4. Planned and complete
5. Unmistakably clear

O. Types of Directions
1. Demands or direct orders
2. Requests
3. Suggestion or implication
4. volunteering

P. Controls
A typical listing of the overall areas in which the supervisor should establish controls might be:
1. Manpower
2. Materials
3. Quality of work
4. Quantity of work
5. Time
6. Space
7. Money
8. Methods

Q. Orienting the New Employee
1. Prepare for him
2. Welcome the new employee
3. Orientation for the job
4. Follow-up

R. Checklist for Orienting New Employees   Yes   No
1. Do you appreciate the feelings of new employees
   when they first report for work?   ___   ___
2. Are you aware of the fact that the new employee must
   make a big adjustment to his job?   ___   ___
3. Have you given him good reasons for liking the job and
   the organization?   ___   ___
4. Have you prepared for his first day on the job?   ___   ___
5. Did you welcome him cordially and make him feel needed?   ___   ___

	Yes	No

6. Did you establish rapport with him so that he feels free to talk and discuss matters with you? ___ ___
7. Did you explain his job to him and his relationship to you? ___ ___
8. Does he know that his work will be evaluated periodically on a basis that is fair and objective? ___ ___
9. Did you introduce him to his fellow workers in such a way that they are likely to accept him? ___ ___
10. Does he know what employee benefits he will receive? ___ ___
11. Does he understand the importance of being on the job and what to do if he must leave his duty station? ___ ___
12. Has he been impressed with the importance of accident prevention and safe practice? ___ ___
13. Does he generally know his way around the department? ___ ___
14. Is he under the guidance of a sponsor who will teach the right way of doing things? ___ ___
15. Do you plan to follow-up so that he will continue to adjust successfully to his job? ___ ___

S. Principles of Learning
  1. Motivation
  2. Demonstration or explanation
  3. Practice

T. Causes of Poor Performance
  1. Improper training for job
  2. Wrong tools
  3. Inadequate directions
  4. Lack of supervisory follow-up
  5. Poor communications
  6. Lack of standards of performance
  7. Wrong work habits
  8. Low morale
  9. Other

U. Four Major Steps in On-The-Job Instruction
  1. Prepare the worker
  2. Present the operation
  3. Tryout performance
  4. Follow-up

V. Employees Want Five Things
  1. Security
  2. Opportunity
  3. Recognition
  4. Inclusion
  5. Expression

W. Some Don'ts in Regard to Praise
1. Don't praise a person for something he hasn't done.
2. Don't praise a person unless you can be sincere.
3. Don't be sparing in praise just because your superior withholds it from you.
4. Don't let too much time elapse between good performance and recognition of it

X. How to Gain Your Workers' Confidence
Methods of developing confidence include such things as:
1. Knowing the interests, habits, hobbies of employees
2. Admitting your own inadequacies
3. Sharing and telling of confidence in others
4. Supporting people when they are in trouble
5. Delegating matters that can be well handled
6. Being frank and straightforward about problems and working conditions
7. Encouraging others to bring their problems to you
8. Taking action on problems which impede worker progress

Y. Sources of Employee Problems
On-the-job causes might be such things as:
1. A feeling that favoritism is exercised in assignments
2. Assignment of overtime
3. An undue amount of supervision
4. Changing methods or systems
5. Stealing of ideas or trade secrets
6. Lack of interest in job
7. Threat of reduction in force
8. Ignorance or lack of communications
9. Poor equipment
10. Lack of knowing how supervisor feels toward employee
11. Shift assignments

Off-the-job problems might have to do with:
1. Health
2. Finances
3. Housing
4. Family

Z. The Supervisor's Key to Discipline
There are several key points about discipline which the supervisor should keep in mind:
1. Job discipline is one of the disciplines of life and is directed by the supervisor.
2. It is more important to correct an employee fault than to fix blame for it.
3. Employee performance is affected by problems both on the job and off.
4. Sudden or abrupt changes in behavior can be indications of important employee problems.
5. Problems should be dealt with as soon as possible after they are identified.
6. The attitude of the supervisor may have more to do with solving problems than the techniques of problem solving.
7. Correction of employee behavior should be resorted to only after the supervisor is sure that training or counseling will not be helpful.

8. Be sure to document your disciplinary actions.
9. Make sure that you are disciplining on the basis of facts rather than personal feelings.
10. Take each disciplinary step in order, being careful not to make snap judgments, or decisions based on impatience.

AA. Five Important Processes of Management
1. Planning
2. Organizing
3. Scheduling
4. Controlling
5. Motivating

BB. When the Supervisor Fails to Plan
1. Supervisor creates impression of not knowing his job
2. May lead to excessive overtime
3. Job runs itself—supervisor lacks control
4. Deadlines and appointments missed
5. Parts of the work go undone
6. Work interrupted by emergencies
7. Sets a bad example
8. Uneven workload creates peaks and valleys
9. Too much time on minor details at expense of more important tasks

CC. Fourteen General Principles of Management
1. Division of work
2. Authority and responsibility
3. Discipline
4. Unity of command
5. Unity of direction
6. Subordination of individual interest to general interest
7. Remuneration of personnel
8. Centralization
9. Scalar chain
10. Order
11. Equity
12. Stability of tenure of personnel
13. Initiative
14. Esprit de corps

DD. Change

Bringing about change is perhaps attempted more often, and yet less well understood, than anything else the supervisor does. How do people generally react to change? (People tend to resist change that is imposed upon them by other individuals or circumstances.

Change is characteristic of every situation. It is a part of every real endeavor where the efforts of people are concerned.

1. Why do people resist change?
   People may resist change because of:
   a. Fear of the unknown
   b. Implied criticism
   c. Unpleasant experiences in the past
   d. Fear of loss of status
   e. Threat to the ego
   f. Fear of loss of economic stability

2. How can we best overcome the resistance to change?
   In initiating change, take these steps:
   a. Get ready to sell
   b. Identify sources of help
   c. Anticipate objections
   d. Sell benefits
   e. Listen in depth
   f. Follow up

II. Brief Topical Summaries

   A. Who/What is the Supervisor?
      1. The supervisor is often called the "highest level employee and the lowest level manager."
      2. A supervisor is a member of both management and the work group. He acts as a bridge between the two.
      3. Most problems in supervision are in the area of human relations, or people problems.
      4. Employees expect: Respect, opportunity to learn and to advance, and a sense of belonging, and so forth.
      5. Supervisors are responsible for directing people and organizing work. Planning is of paramount importance.
      6. A position description is a set of duties and responsibilities inherent to a given position.
      7. It is important to keep the position description up-to-date and to provide each employee with his own copy.

   B. The Sociology of Work
      1. People are alike in many ways; however, each individual is unique.
      2. The supervisor is challenged in getting to know employee differences. Acquiring skills in evaluating individuals is an asset.
      3. Maintaining meaningful working relationships in the organization is of great importance.
      4. The supervisor has an obligation to help individuals to develop to their fullest potential.
      5. Job rotation on a planned basis helps to build versatility and to maintain interest and enthusiasm in work groups.
      6. Cross training (job rotation) provides backup skills.

7. The supervisor can help reduce tension by maintaining a sense of humor, providing guidance to employees, and by making reasonable and timely decisions. Employees respond favorably to working under reasonably predictable circumstances.
8. Change is characteristic of all managerial behavior. The supervisor must adjust to changes in procedures, new methods, technological changes, and to a number of new and sometimes challenging situations.
9. To overcome the natural tendency for people to resist change, the supervisor should become more skillful in initiating change.

C. Principles and Practices of Supervision
1. Employees should be required to answer to only one superior.
2. A supervisor can effectively direct only a limited number of employees, depending upon the complexity, variety, and proximity of the jobs involved.
3. The organizational chart presents the organization in graphic form. It reflects lines of authority and responsibility as well as interrelationships of units within the organization.
4. Distribution of work can be improved through an analysis using the "Work Distribution Chart."
5. The "Work Distribution Chart" reflects the division of work within a unit in understandable form.
6. When related tasks are given to an employee, he has a better chance of increasing his skills through training.
7. The individual who is given the responsibility for tasks must also be given the appropriate authority to insure adequate results.
8. The supervisor should delegate repetitive, routine work. Preparation of recurring reports, maintaining leave and attendance records are some examples.
9. Good discipline is essential to good task performance. Discipline is reflected in the actions of employees on the job in the absence of supervision.
10. Disciplinary action may have to be taken when the positive aspects of discipline have failed. Reprimand, warning, and suspension are examples of disciplinary action.
11. If a situation calls for a reprimand, be sure it is deserved and remember it is to be done in private.

D. Dynamic Leadership
1. A style is a personal method or manner of exerting influence.
2. Authoritarian leaders often see themselves as the source of power and authority.
3. The democratic leader often perceives the group as the source of authority and power.
4. Supervisors tend to do better when using the pattern of leadership that is most natural for them.
5. Social scientists suggest that the effective supervisor use the leadership style that best fits the problem or circumstances involved.
6. All four styles—telling, selling, consulting, joining—have their place. Using one does not preclude using the other at another time.

7. The theory X point of view assumes that the average person dislikes work, will avoid it whenever possible, and must be coerced to achieve organizational objectives.
8. The theory Y point of view assumes that the average person considers work to be a natural as play, and, when the individual is committed, he requires little supervision or direction to accomplish desired objectives.
9. The leader's basic assumptions concerning human behavior and human nature affect his actions, decisions, and other managerial practices.
10. Dissatisfaction among employees is often present, but difficult to isolate. The supervisor should seek to weaken dissatisfaction by keeping promises, being sincere and considerate, keeping employees informed, and so forth.
11. Constructive suggestions should be encouraged during the natural progress of the work.

E. Processes for Solving Problems
1. People find their daily tasks more meaningful and satisfying when they can improve them.
2. The causes of problems, or the key factors, are often hidden in the background. Ability to solve problems often involves the ability to isolate them from their backgrounds. There is some substance to the cliché that some persons "can't see the forest for the trees."
3. New procedures are often developed from old ones. Problems should be broken down into manageable parts. New ideas can be adapted from old one.
4. People think differently in problem-solving situations. Using a logical, patterned approach is often useful. One approach found to be useful includes these steps:
   a. Define the problem
   b. Establish objectives
   c. Get the facts
   d. Weigh and decide
   e. Take action
   f. Evaluate action

F. Training for Results
1. Participants respond best when they feel training is important to them.
2. The supervisor has responsibility for the training and development of those who report to him.
3. When training is delegated to others, great care must be exercised to insure the trainer has knowledge, aptitude, and interest for his work as a trainer.
4. Training (learning) of some type goes on continually. The most successful supervisor makes certain the learning contributes in a productive manner to operational goals.
5. New employees are particularly susceptible to training. Older employees facing new job situations require specific training, as well as having need for development and growth opportunities.
6. Training needs require continuous monitoring.
7. The training officer of an agency is a professional with a responsibility to assist supervisors in solving training problems.

8. Many of the self-development steps important to the supervisor's own growth are equally important to the development of peers and subordinates. Knowledge of these is important when the supervisor consults with others on development and growth opportunities.

G. Health, Safety, and Accident Prevention
1. Management-minded supervisors take appropriate measures to assist employees in maintaining health and in assuring safe practices in the work environment.
2. Effective safety training and practices help to avoid injury and accidents.
3. Safety should be a management goal. All infractions of safety which are observed should be corrected without exception.
4. Employees' safety attitude, training and instruction, provision of safe tools and equipment, supervision, and leadership are considered highly important factors which contribute to safety and which can be influenced directly by supervisors.
5. When accidents do occur, they should be investigated promptly for very important reasons, including the fact that information which is gained can be used to prevent accidents in the future.

H. Equal Employment Opportunity
1. The supervisor should endeavor to treat all employees fairly, without regard to religion, race, sex, or national origin.
2. Groups tend to reflect the attitude of the leader. Prejudice can be detected even in very subtle form. Supervisors must strive to create a feeling of mutual respect and confidence in every employee.
3. Complete utilization of all human resources is a national goal. Equitable consideration should be accorded women in the work force, minority-group members, the physically and mentally handicapped, and the older employee. The important question is: "Who can do the job?"
4. Training opportunities, recognition for performance, overtime assignments, promotional opportunities, and all other personnel actions are to be handled on an equitable basis.

I. Improving Communications
1. Communications is achieving understanding between the sender and the receiver of a message. It also means sharing information—the creation of understanding.
2. Communication is basic to all human activity. Words are means of conveying meanings; however, real meanings are in people.
3. There are very practical differences in the effectiveness of one-way, impersonal, and two-way communications. Words spoken face-to-face are better understood. Telephone conversations are effective, but lack the rapport of person-to-person exchanges. The whole person communicates.
4. Cooperation and communication in an organization go hand in hand. When there is a mutual respect between people, spelling out rules and procedures for communicating is unnecessary.
5. There are several barriers to effective communications. These include failure to listen with respect and understanding, lack of skill in feedback, and misinterpreting the meanings of words used by the speaker. It is also common

practice to listen to what we want to hear, and tune out things we do not want to hear.
6. Communication is management's chief problem. The supervisor should accept the challenge to communicate more effectively and to improve interagency and intra-agency communications.
7. The supervisor may often plan for and conduct meetings. The planning phase is critical and may determine the success or the failure of a meeting.
8. Speaking before groups usually requires extra effort. Stage fright may never disappear completely, but it can be controlled.

J. Self-Development
1. Every employee is responsible for his own self-development.
2. Toastmaster and toastmistress clubs offer opportunities to improve skills in oral communications.
3. Planning for one's own self-development is of vital importance. Supervisors know their own strengths and limitations better than anyone else.
4. Many opportunities are open to aid the supervisor in his developmental efforts, including job assignments; training opportunities, both governmental and non-governmental—to include universities and professional conferences and seminars.
5. Programmed instruction offers a means of studying at one's own rate.
6. Where difficulties may arise from a supervisor's being away from his work for training, he may participate in televised home study or correspondence courses to meet his self-development needs.

K. Teaching and Training
1. The Teaching Process
Teaching is encouraging and guiding the learning activities of students toward established goals. In most cases this process consists of five steps: preparation, presentation, summarization, evaluation, and application.

   a. Preparation
   Preparation is two-fold in nature; that of the supervisor and the employee. Preparation by the supervisor is absolutely essential to success. He must know what, when, where, how, and whom he will teach. Some of the factors that should be considered are:
   1) The objectives
   2) The materials needed
   3) The methods to be used
   4) Employee participation
   5) Employee interest
   6) Training aids
   7) Evaluation
   8) Summarization

   Employee preparation consists in preparing the employee to receive the material. Probably the most important single factor in the preparation of the employee is arousing and maintaining his interest. He must know the objectives of the training, why he is there, how the material can be used, and its importance to him.

b. Presentation
   In presentation, have a carefully designed plan and follow it. The plan should be accurate and complete, yet flexible enough to meet situations as they arise. The method of presentation will be determined by the particular situation and objectives.

c. Summary
   A summary should be made at the end of every training unit and program. In addition, there may be internal summaries depending on the nature of the material being taught. The important thing is that the trainee must always be able to understand how each part of the new material relates to the whole.

d. Application
   The supervisor must arrange work so the employee will be given a chance to apply new knowledge or skills while the material is still clear in his mind and interest is high. The trainee does not really know whether he has learned the material until he has been given a chance to apply it. If the material is not applied, it loses most of its value.

e. Evaluation
   The purpose of all training is to promote learning. To determine whether the training has been a success or failure, the supervisor must evaluate this learning.
   In the broadest sense, evaluation includes all the devices, methods, skills, and techniques used by the supervisor to keep himself and the employees informed as to their progress toward the objectives they are pursuing. The extent to which the employee has mastered the knowledge, skills, and abilities, or changed his attitudes, as determined by the program objectives, is the extent to which instruction has succeeded or failed.
   Evaluation should not be confined to the end of the lesson, day, or program but should be used continuously. We shall note later the way this relates to the rest of the teaching process.

2. Teaching Methods
   A teaching method is a pattern of identifiable student and instructor activity used in presenting training material.
   All supervisors are faced with the problem of deciding which method should be used at a given time.

   a. Lecture
      The lecture is direct oral presentation of material by the supervisor. The present trend is to place less emphasis on the trainer's activity and more on that of the trainee.

   b. Discussion
      Teaching by discussion or conference involves using questions and other techniques to arouse interest and focus attention upon certain areas, and by doing so creating a learning situation. This can be one of the most

valuable methods because it gives the employees an opportunity to express their ideas and pool their knowledge.

    c. Demonstration
The demonstration is used to teach how something works or how to do something. It can be used to show a principle or what the results of a series of actions will be. A well-staged demonstration is particularly effective because it shows proper methods of performance in a realistic manner.

    d. Performance
Performance is one of the most fundamental of all learning techniques or teaching methods. The trainee may be able to tell how a specific operation should be performed but he cannot be sure he knows how to perform the operation until he has done so.
As with all methods, there are certain advantages and disadvantages to each method.

    e. Which Method to Use
Moreover, there are other methods and techniques of teaching. It is difficult to use any method without other methods entering into it. In any learning situation, a combination of methods is usually more effective than any one method alone.

Finally, evaluation must be integrated into the other aspects of the teaching-learning process.

It must be used in the motivation of the trainees; it must be used to assist in developing understanding during the training; and it must be related to employee application of the results of training.

This is distinctly the role of the supervisor.

USE AND CARE OF EQUIPMENT, MATERIALS, AND SUPPLIES

TABLE OF CONTENTS

		Page
I.	GENERAL POINTS TO BE OBSERVED	1
II.	USE AND CARE OF NON-AUTOMATIC/MANUAL EQUIPMENT	3
III.	USE AND CARE OF AUTOMATIC EQUIPMENT	8
IV.	HELPFUL SERVICE HINTS FOR WET AND DRY VACUUM	11
V.	HELPFUL SERVICE HINTS FOR FLOOR MACHINES	13
VI.	HELPFUL SERVICE HINTS FOR AUTOMATIC SCRUBBERS	14

USE AND CARE OF EQUIPMENT, MATERIALS, AND SUPPLIES

I. GENERAL POINTS TO BE OBSERVED

The institution has invested a large amount of money in expensive modern equipment, materials, and supplies in order to help fulfill the housekeeping goals. Therefore, it is the responsibility of each employee to keep the equipment in good working condition and use materials and supplies economically.

Storing of equipment is part of the housekeeping aid's job in caring for equipment. Some institutions have storage areas or utility rooms located in each department or on each floor. Others have central equipment rooms near the housekeeper's office. These areas are equipped with hooks, racks, shelves, sinks, and floor drains for the cleaning and storing of equipment, materials, and supplies.

The storage area must be maintained daily and every item must have a place.

Care of equipment, materials, and supplies are divided into two groups: care of non-automatic/manual equipment, and care of power-operated (electric or battery) equipment. However, there are several general points to be observed on the care and upkeep of all equipment, materials, and supplies.

1. Follow manufacturer's instructions for operation and maintenance.

2. Provide a preventive maintenance program (routine and systematic inspections and repairs).

3. Replace equipment, materials, or supplies promptly when faulty or ineffective.

4. Keep equipment clean at all times.

5. Use materials and supplies economically.

6. Provide adequate and proper storage area for equipment, materials, and supplies.

7. Use each piece of equipment only for its intended purpose.

8. Report faulty, damaged, or ineffective materials or equipment to the supervisor.

PURPOSE: To maintain equipment in good working condition; to insure faster, easier, and more efficient performance; to control bacteria and for appearance.

EQUIPMENT:
    Germicidal detergent
    Cloths or sponges
    Buckets (two)
    Gloves

2

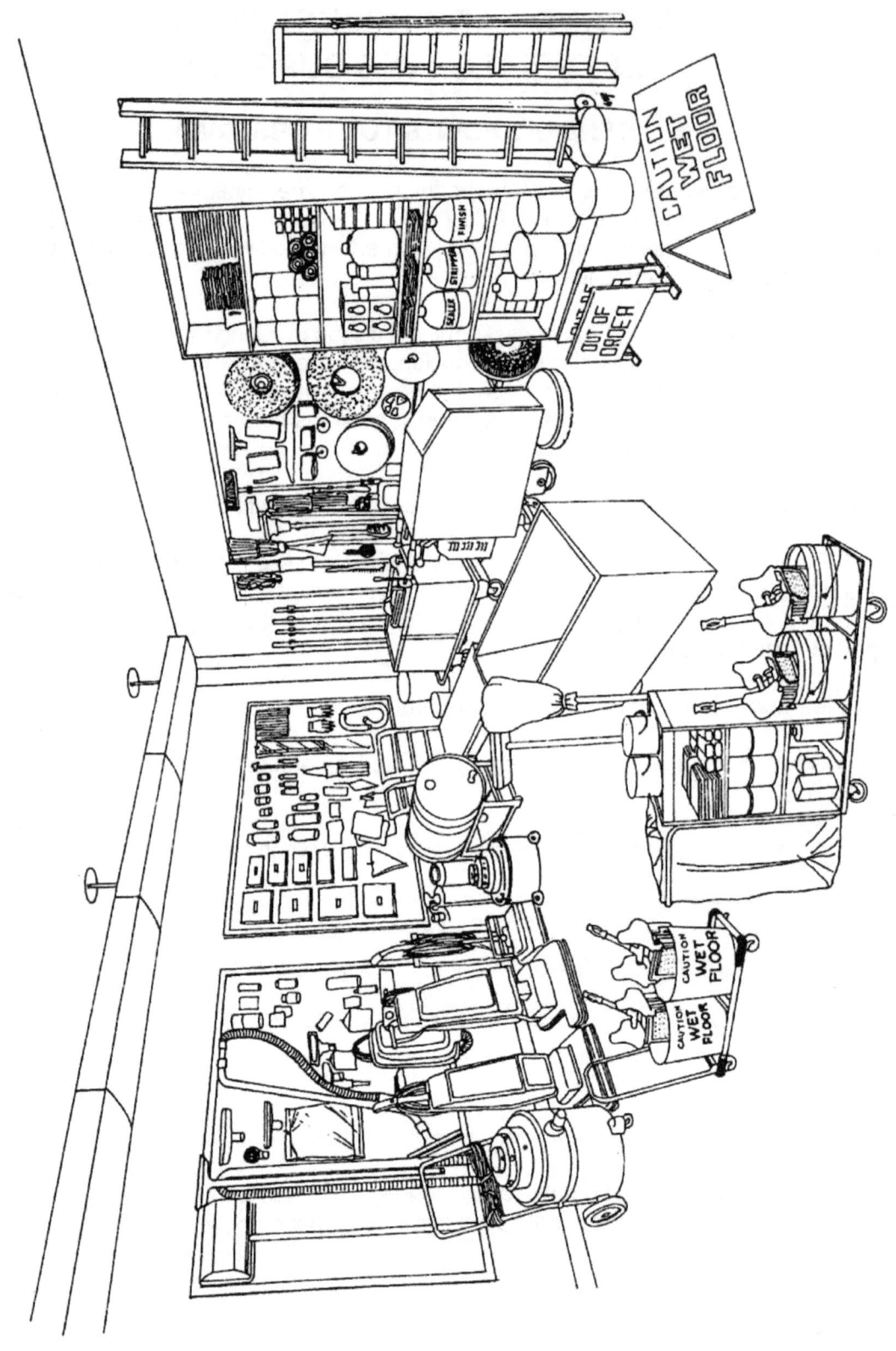

SAFETY PRECAUTIONS:

1. Never pour used sealer or finish back into clean solution containers.

2. Brushes should never be stored on the bristles or left on machines.

3. Do not use more of an item than is necessary to efficiently perform the task.

4. Make sure pressure is released from wall washing tanks before cleaning.

5. All equipment must be cleaned at the end of the day and returned to designated storage area.

II. USE AND CARE OF NON-AUTOMATIC/MANUAL EQUIPMENT

Included in this type of equipment are items used in housekeeping duties that are entirely moved or operated by hand. This includes everything from brushes to wall washing pressure tanks.

EQUIPMENT:
- Utility carts
- Brushes of all types:
    a. Counter
    b. Sweeping
    c. Toilet
    d. Deck and other scrub brushes
    e. Radiator
    f. Scrub and polish
    g. Pot
    h. Nylon hand brush
    i. Coving or baseboard
- Dustpans
- Screens, sifters, and slit spoons
- Caution signs
- Squeegees
- Buckets (small and large)
- Dollies
- Wringers
- Mopheads
- Nylon pads
- Sweeping floor tools
- Extension handles
- Trash carts
- Wall washing pressure tanks
- Ladders
- Gloves
- Sealers
- Strippers (bulk and portioned)
- Finishes (bulk and portioned)
- Germicidal detergents (bulk and portioned)
- Polishes (furniture, stainless steel)
- Treated cloths
- Dust cloths
- Soaps
- Plastic liners
- Carpet sweepers
- Putty knives
- Hose (water)
- Measuring cups
- Mopping tanks
- Spray units
- Toilet tissue
- Paper towels
- Bottles (plastic)
- Trash containers
- Corn brooms

PROCEDURE

Utility Carts

1. Wipe off all shelves with germicidal cloth at the end of the day. Dry.
2. Place plastic liner on top shelf to keep from rusting.
3. Use it daily in performing duties as assigned.
4. Keep shelves neatly stocked with all supplies and equipment.

Brushes

1. Clean at the end of the day.
2. Comb with a stiff fiber brush or comb and wash under running water. Shake out excess water.
3. Store by hanging on rack, free from touching any surface or store on block/wood part of the brush.
4. Do not use until bristles are dry.
5. For maximum wear and effectiveness, brushes with removable handles should be rotated at least once a week.
6. Always hang broom up. Never stand on the straws.

Bottles (Plastic Spray Bottle)

1. Clean exterior with paper towel dipped in germicidal solution. Dry.
2. Return to utility cart.
3. A trigger type must be taken apart regularly and washed and rinsed thoroughly.

Carpet Sweepers

1. Empty into plastic liner after each use. Place liner in trash collection container.
2. Remove strings and debris from brush and wheel.
3. Damp wipe the sweeper.

Caution Signs (Wet Floor, Out of Order)

1. Damp wipe and dry after each use.
2. Periodically, thoroughly wash, rinse, and dry.

Cloths (Treated and Cleaning)

1. Treated
   a. Use all surfaces of the woven treated paper before discarding.
   b. Treat own cloths by spraying lightly with solution and allow to stand overnight in covered container. May be discarded or laundered.
2. Cleaning:
   a. Rinse frequently during use.
   b. At the end of the day or at the end of the bathroom cleaning procedure, place cleaning cloths in plastic liner, then put into a regular laundry bag for laundering.
   c. Never leave cloths lying around.

Dustpans

1. Clean at the end of the day. Wash with germicidal solution.
2. Rinse and dry.
3. Hang on hook on cart so that it will not become bent or damaged.

Extension Handles

1. Use as an aid for high dusting.
2. Wipe off daily.

Floor Sweeping Tools

1. Use a disposable cloth.
2. Use all surfaces possible.
3. Damp wipe handle and foot frame daily.
4. Wash tool once a week with germicidal detergent.
5. Hang up on utility cart when not in use.

Germicidal Detergents and Strippers

1. Used in the cleaning operation to remove soil.
2. Do not overuse—will destroy flooring surfaces.
3. Use recommended amount only.
4. Read label before using.

Gloves

1. Wash outside of gloves under running water (while on hand) at the end of the day.
2. Remove and wash inside. Wipe dry.
3. Hang across a smooth surface to dry.

Hose (With Cut-off Nozzle)

1. Rinse off rubber or plastic hose.
2. Roll in a three-foot circle to prevent kinking. Drain water while rolling.
3. Hang hose on a rack or peg in storage area.

Knives (Putty—Short and Long)

1. Wipe handle and blade with germicidal solution at end of day. Dry.
2. Return to cart.

Ladders (Safety and Platform)

1. Wipe off after each use with germicidal solution.
2. Rinse and dry.
3. Return to designated storage area.

Measuring Cups

1. Rinse immediately after use.
2. Dry.
3. Store so that it will not be damaged.

Mops—Dust

1. Do not use to mop up spills.
2. Remove loose soil from mop frequently, by vacuum if possible.
3. Remove mophead at end of day, place in plastic bag and take to designated storage area for laundering.

Mops—Wet

1. Cut off loose and uneven yarn strands.
2. Never twist or squeeze mop extra hard; such action will break fibers and destroy the mophead.
3. Remove mophead at the end of bathroom cleaning and at the end of the day.
4. Place in plastic bag and into laundry bag and take to designated storage area for laundering.

Mopping Tanks, Buckets, Wringers, and Dollies

1. Remove any loose mophead yarn, string, or foreign matter.
2. Wash, rinse, and dry daily. Invert small and medium size buckets to dry.
3. Keep the equipment in good repair. Report any defects to supervisor.
4. When necessary, add a few drops of oil to casters.
5. Avoid hitting the mopping unit against other objects and walls.
6. Replace bumper strip when needed.
7. Do not allow a cleaning solution to remain in the bucket when the bucket is not in use.

Small Buckets or Pails

1. Empty contents.
2. Wash, rinse, and dry.
3. Turn upside down to dry.

Polishes

1. Used on furniture, stainless steel, wood, and metal.
2. Use only the recommended amount.
3. It is very annoying to get polish on one's clothes, so thoroughly rub the surface to remove excess polish.

Paper Towels and Toilet Tissue

1. Replacement supplies.
2. Always place in containers, not in window sills or on top of cabinets.

Screens, Sifters/Slit Spoons

1. Wash and shake off excess water.
2. Dry. Handle so as not to bend screen.
3. Place on hook on utility cart or other designated storage area.

Nylon Pads

1. Wash pads under running water. Rinse.
2. Hang or store on flat surface until dry.

Plastic Liners

1. Used to line trash containers.
2. Must be replaced daily.
3. Do not use for any other purpose than intended.

Sealers, Finishers

1. Items used to protect flooring.
2. These items are very expensive.
3. Use liners in buckets when using sealer and finish.
4. Never pour solution on floor.
5. Wipe up spills or drips immediately.
6. Never waste the product. Pour just enough on mophead in bucket to wet mophead, which should eliminate any material being left over.
7. In case there is a small amount left over, discard it. Do not pour into clean solution; solution will sour.
8. Mopheads should be placed in plastic liner/bag for laundering.
9. Wash, rinse, and dry buckets, wringers, dolly, mops, and mop handles used in these operations.

Soaps

1. Used for hand washing and bathing.
2. Must rinse before using.
3. Not used for cleaning inanimate surfaces

Sponges

1. Place in germicidal solution. Wash thoroughly. Squeeze out excess water.
2. Rinse. Squeeze out excess water.
3. Place on flat surface to dry. Do not hang on nails.

Squeegees (Small or Large)

1. Wash squeegee blades in germicidal solution.
2. Rinse. Drain off excess water.
3. Wipe dry and return to utility cart or storage area.
4. Do not store with squeegee blades down.

Spray Units

1. Used for spray buffing and dry stripping.
2. Wipe off with germicidal solution.
3. Rinse spray nozzles.
4. Do not let material harden on nozzle.

Trash Containers

1. Used to receive or hold waste.
2. Handle containers so as not to scratch, puncture, or bend them.
3. Wipe trash container inside and out daily. Replace liner.
4. Once a month, collect trash containers, take to utility room, and thoroughly wash, rinse, and dry or steam clean.

Trash Carts

1. Used for general collection of trash.
2. Take to utility room. Wash inside and outside thoroughly. Let drain.
3. Rinse and let drain.
4. Wipe dry.

Wall Washing Machines/Pressure Tanks

1. Empty at the end of the operation.
2. Rinse tubing and inside of tanks.
3. Wipe off outside with germicidal detergent. Dry.
4. Store in designated storage area.

III. USE AND CARE OF AUTOMATIC EQUIPMENT

Automatic equipment is equipment that is power operated either by electricity or battery. This type of equipment is very expensive and must be properly maintained to insure good service and maximum efficiency. Therefore, keep this equipment free of dirt, and oiled properly, and keep screws and nuts tight. Automatic equipment is usually divided into three categories: floor machines, vacuum cleaners, and automatic scrubbers.

EQUIPMENT:
    Single disc floor machines, with or without spray attachments
    Drive assemblies
    Square buffers—attachments (plates and baseboard scrubbers)
    Shampoo machines
    Vacuums
        a. Suction
        b. Back-Pack
        c. Wet and dry
        d. Pile lifter
        e. Upright

Vacuum attachments (wand, hose, crevice tool, brushes), floor, wall, ceiling, upholstery, carpet and attachments for wet floor operation.
Battery-operated sweepers
Automatic mop assemblies

PROCEDURE

Floor Machines

1. Used for scrubbing, stripping, and polishing of large or small areas quickly. Also used for special application, such as spray buffing and dry stripping.
2. Never attach brush by running machine over it and allowing it to lock.
3. Never leave machine unattended. Disconnect when not in use.
4. Machine is cleaned at the end of the day or after completion of assignment.

    a. At the work site, tilt machine back on handle. Remove brush and pad or drive assembly and place in plastic liners/bags.
    b. Rinse machine in upright position. Damp wipe cord with germicidal cloth. Wind cord on handle or storage hooks as it is being wiped. Inspect for defects and report to supervisor.
    c. Take equipment to utility room. Remove brushes, pads and/or drive assembly from plastic liners/bags. Wash thoroughly under running water. Store on flat surface or hang on peg to dry. DO NOT USE AGAIN UNTIL DRY.
    d. Wash handle and exterior surface of machine. Dry.
    e. Tilt on handle and rinse the underside of the brush housing with clean water. Dry.
    f. If a solution tank is used, rinse tank and feed lines/tubing. Dry.
    g. Store equipment in designated storage area.
    h. Never store machines on brushes. Store in tilted position.

Extension Cords

1. If an extension cord is used, make sure it is the same size as on the equipment so that the proper amount of current is carried to machine.
2. Do not yank on an electric cord to pull the plug from the outlet.
3. Damp wipe cord with germicidal solution. Dry.
4. Wind loosely and hang or lay in a safe place.

Vacuum Cleaners (Upright, Wet and Dry, Back-Pack)

1. Used to remove soil from floors and carpeting, window sills, ledges, screens, vents, blinds, upholstery, walls, and ceiling; and to pick up water—scrub, rinse, overflow, flooding.
2. Empty upright vacuums when bag is half full
    a. Outer bags may be cloth, moleskin, or paper.
    b. Cloth and moleskin bags may be vacuumed, but never washed. Discard disposable bags.
    c. Damp wipe handle, hose, and cord with germicidal solution. Dry.

3. Clean wet and dry vacuum at the end of the day.
    a. If used for dry purposes:
        (1) Make sure machine is set up with flannel and paper liners.

(2) To clean, remove hose, head assembly, and cloth filter. Leave paper filter in place.
(3) Tilt machine back on handle and wheels. Pull out bag so that it hangs outward.
(4) Continue raising machine until it is resting on handle. Slap tank several times to dislodge all dirt.
(5) Remove bag by sliding elastic band off the lip of the tank. Place in a plastic liner. Tie and discard.
(6) Wash tank inside and outside with germicidal solution. Rinse and dry.
(7) Wash all attachments. Rinse and dry.
(8) Wipe off cord and rewind on handle, not around head assembly.
(9) Wipe off head assembly.
(10) Check impaction filter. Not necessary to remove after each usage, unless torn, damaged or wet. Supervisor should set a specific time for changing (for example, every 30 days).
(11) Take equipment to designated storage area. Leave head assembly off tank. Turn on side for airing and drying purposes.

  b. If used for wet purposes:
    (1) Make sure machine is set up for the wet operation.
    (2) Remove flannel and paper liners and insert the cyclonic separator which has a float that shuts off the suction of the machine when tank is filled to maximum level.
    (3) To clean, remove hose, head assembly, and lift out cyclonic separator.
    (4) Wheel machine to area with drain or low sink. Tilt back on handles to empty. (Some of these have drain valves.)
    (5) Rinse two or three times with clean water to remove sludge.
    (6) Wash, rinse, and dry tank and accessories.
    (7) Store in designated storage area.
    (8) If impaction filter is wet, allow to dry. Sterilize or autoclave before using again.

Automatic Scrubbers/Sweepers

Used for scrubbing, stripping, buffing, and sweeping large areas. In order for machines to work properly, they must be charged daily in a well-ventilated room. Battery must be checked regularly and distilled water added when water is below internal plate or triangle. Battery cover must be left opened when charging. Do not smoke in area when machine is being charged.

1. Automatic Scrubber
   a. To clean, take equipment to utility room. Empty; open dump valve or fold tanks over drain.
   b. Flush tanks, wheels, and squeegee. Use a hose to perform this task.
   c. Wash exterior surface with germicidal solution.
   d. Rinse and dry.
   e. Take to designated storage area.
   f. Make sure windows are open.
   g. Report any defects, damages, or necessary repairs to supervisor.

2. Powered Sweeper
   a. To clean, take to utility room. Remove and empty trash pan.
   b. Shake down filters; remove and empty pan.

c. Remove brushes; comb, wash, rinse, and shake well. Dry.
d. Wash exterior surface with germicidal solution. Rinse and dry.
e. Wash pans. Rinse and dry.
f. Replace all parts.
g. Take to designated storage area.
h. Check battery; leave cover open.
i. Connect for charging.
j. Make sure windows are open.
k. Report any defects or necessary repairs to supervisor

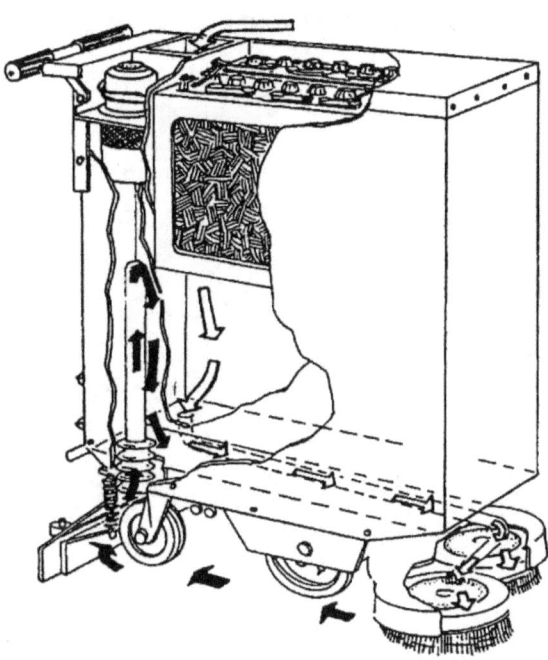
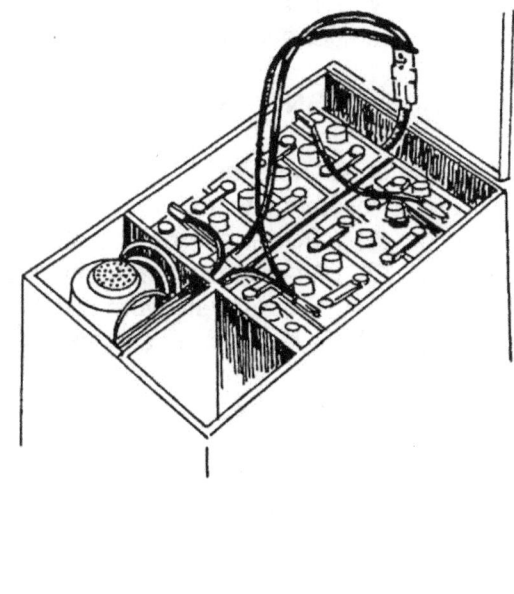

IV. HELPFUL SERVICE HINTS FOR WET AND DRY VACUUM

1. Always operate vacuum on the proper voltages as outlined on the data plate.

2. After using for dry applications, remove the disposable paper bag (5 to 9 gallon units only), and mitten flannel filter and clean before reusing. For added convenience, keep a supply of disposable paper bags on hand (5 and 9 gallon units only; they may be obtained from your authorized distributor.

3. If air movement is interrupted in your vacuum, check the dust filter to make sure it's clean. To see if hose has become clogged, remove hose from machine and test suction at machine intake. Sometimes a clogged tool will be the culprit, so check tools periodically.

4. For wet work, remove the disposable paper bag and dust filter, then place the water separator in the tank (5 and 9 gallon units only). In the 10 gallon models, install the wet filter and water shut-off.

5. After using machine for wet work, and before putting it away, clean tank inside and outside; clean tools thoroughly.

6. Store machinery in clean dry place.

7. The suds suppressor bar at the tank inlet should be checked and replaced, if necessary, after 125 gallons of solution have been picked up. Suds suppressor bar is replaced by removing inlet deflector and sliding new bar into place. These bars may be obtained from authorized distributor (for 5 and 9 gallon units only).

8. Many tools are available for the wet and dry vacuum. Contact your authorized distributor for additional tools.

SERVICE DIAGNOSIS:

1. Motor will not start
   a. Possible causes:
      (1) Power source or outlet dead
      (2) Vacuum switch faulty or damaged
      (3) Excessively worn brushes
      (4) Wire shorted or broken

   b. How to correct:
      (1) Activate source or check cord
      (2) Replace switch
      (3) Replace brushes
      (4) Replace wires

2. Little or no suction
   a. Possible causes:
      (1) Full tank; wet shut-off closes fan inlet
      (2) Clogged attachment inlet, hose or vacuum inlet
      (3) Clogged filter bag
      (4) Tank gasket seal leaks
      (5) Exhaust air outlet covered

   b. How to correct:
      (1) Empty tank
      (2) Remove lodged materials
      (3) Clean filter bag
      (4) Position seal properly
      (5) Remove obstruction

3. Machine noisy
   a. Possible causes:
      (1) Vibration or resonating of metal parts
      (2) Dirty filter

b. How to correct:
   (1) Secure all mountings firmly
   (2) Clean filter

4. Motor runs hot or smells warm
   a. Possible causes:
      (1) Motor cooling air intake or exhaust clogged
      (2) Motor overloaded with mist or suds
      (3) Dirty filter

   b. How to correct:
      (1) Clean air intake and exhaust passages
      (2) Empty tank; install new suds suppressor
      (3) Clean filter

V. HELPFUL SERVICE HINTS FOR FLOOR MACHINES

SERVICE DIAGNOSIS:

1. Machine wobbles; hard to control
   a. Possible causes:
      (1) Brush bristles distorted resulting in brush being uneven
      (2) Switch housing not tight on handle tube
      (3) Handle tube not connected firmly to machine hose
      (4) Pads or brushes worn unevenly

   b. How to correct:
      (1) If brush is new, soak in water for several hours; remove from water; shake off excess water; rest brush on flat surface on back with bristles pointing upward.
      (2) Tighten bolts securing housing to handle tube; tighten set screws. If housing is still loose, drill and tap new hole in housing, insert pointed set screw and tighten firmly.
      (3) Check all mounting bolts for tightness; insert washers for shims if necessary.
      (4) Replace with new pad or brush.

2. Motor will not run
   a. Possible causes:
      (1) Unplugged at wall
      (2) Unplugged between motor and handle cable.
      (3) Fuse blown or circuit breaker tripped
      (4) Cable wires severed
      (5) Switch burned out
      (6) Wires detached at switch
      (7) Motor burned out

   b. How to correct; follow these steps:
      (1) Visibly check all connections to be sure the plugs are securely plugged into the appropriate receptacle.
      (2) Check fuse or circuit breaker. Replace or reset if necessary.

(3) Visibly and carefully check cable for wire breakage.
(4) Unplug motor from handle cable and connect motor directly to wall receptacle through use of an adequate gauge extension cord (at least 14-2). CAUTION: Remove brush or pad holder from machine before plugging into power source.
(5) If after #4 above motor does not operate, remove motor from machine and take it to your distributor, or an electrical repair station designated by your distributor for repairs.
(6) If after #4 above does operate, the problem lies between the motor and the wall receptacle. Remove switch box cover plate and ascertain that al electrical connections are secure.
(7) Remove cable from the terminals on the switch and replace with an extension cord (preferably 14-3) to determine if wires have been severed inside the cable.
(8) Replace switch.

3. Runs hot
   a. Possible causes:
      (1) Motor overloaded. Machine does not have sufficient power for the job. (Example: dry spray-buff cleaning with abrasive pad.)
      (2) Air intake ducts clogged with dust and lint.

   b. How to correct:
      (1) Secure the proper machine for the job or use the same machine with pads of less abrasive material.
      (2) Remove drip cover and shroud. Use forced air to blow dust and lint from motor.

VI. HELPFUL SERVICE HINTS FOR AUTOMATIC SCRUBBERS

SERVICE DIAGNOSIS:

1. Motor will not start
   a. Possible causes:
      (1) Battery charge condition very low; check with hydrometer
      (2) Battery connectors loose or disconnected
      (3) Loose or broken wires

   b. How to correct:
      (1) Recharge batteries fully before beginning operations
      (2) Fasten battery connections securely
      (3) Fasten all wires securely and tape

2. Machine will not move
   a. Possible causes:
      (1) Clutch requires adjusting
      (2) "V" belt slipping
      (3) Battery charge condition very low; check with hydrometer

    b. How to correct:
        (1) Adjust clutch per "Clutch Adjustment" instructions
        (2) Adjust "V" belt tightness
        (3) Recharge batteries fully before beginning operations

3. Machine streaking a cleaned floor
    a. Possible causes:
        (1) Foreign materials lodged under rear squeegee blade
        (2) Insufficient water flow to brushes
        (3) Worn squeegee blades
        (4) Squeegee out of adjustment
        (5) Worn brushes or pads

    b. How to correct:
        (1) Raise squeegee and clean squeegee blade
        (2) Clean fine filter screen in tank and examine lines for a flow restriction
        (3) Replace squeegee blade
        (4) Adjust per instructions
        (5) Replace brushes or pads

4. Solution not being properly picked up
    a. Possible causes:
        (1) Vacuum motor wired for 12 or 18 volts and too much solution being laid
        (2) Clogged pick-up tube
        (3) Air leaks around vacuum motor mount
        (4) Ball check (water shut-off) sealing vacuum motor opening to tank
        (5) Clogged filters
        (6) Drain valve not completely closed
        (7) Pick-up tube plug or suds suppressors not seated properly

    b. How to correct:
        (1) Use 24-volt switch position
        (2) Remove lint accumulations and clean tube through plugged hole in tank at top of tube
        (3) Seal all leaks
        (4) Clean ball check (water shut-off) assembly
        (5) Replace filters
        (6) Close valve
        (7) Securely seat pick-up tube plug

5. Short operating time
    a. Possible causes:
        (1) Battery charge condition very low; check with hydrometer
        (2) Continuous heavy motor load due to special brushes
        (3) Constant brush operation; 210 lb. position

    b. How to correct:
        (1) Recharge batteries fully before beginning operations
        (2) Use special brushes requiring heavy motor load only for particular application
        (3) Use locked brush cleaning operations sparingly

6. Machine pulls to one side
   a. Possible causes
      (1) Squeegee dragging only on one side

   b. How to correct:
      (1) Adjust per instructions

7. Machine creeps
   a. Possible causes:
      (1) Clutch out of proper adjustment
      (2) Clutch cable binding in wound wire casing
      (3) Clutch collar sticking

   b. How to correct:
      (1) Adjust clutch per "Clutch Adjustment" instructions
      (2) Lubricate clutch cable and casing
      (3) Lubricate clutch